SPIRIT GUIDES ON SPEED DIAL **WORKBOOK**

Jules Apollo

UTOPIAN
FOREST

Published 2024 by Utopian Forest, an imprint of Jules Apollo LLC
Printed in the United States of America

ISBN: 979-8-9891599-2-5 (paperback)

Interior design by Choi Messer
Cover design by 100Covers

CONTENTS

INTRODUCTION

THIS WORKBOOK IS INTENDED AS a companion to the *Spirit Guides on Speed Dial* book. It can be used on its own as it includes the scripts and exercises from the book, but lacks the stories, channeled messages from the guides, and some background context for the material.

Parts 2 and 3 are bonus sections for the workbook, they aren't included in *Spirit Guides on Speed Dial*.

Part 1: Creating Your Practice includes details from each chapter in the book. Lined space is provided for answering questions, with open pages available for sketching, writing, painting, and/or using stickers as you explore working with your guides.

Part 2: Playing and Experimenting is provided for playful experimentation and introspection to strengthen your partnership with your guides and your intuition and soul.

Part 3: Unfurling and Expanding is for deeper exploration of your spiritual practice and work with your guides.

Closure is the end of this beginning of your journey with your guides and includes brief thoughts on continuing your unfurling and expansion into the fullness of your soul's strengths and partnership with your guides.

Additional materials can be found at https://julesapollo.com and https://julesapollo.substack.com.

May your relationship with your guides bring you comfort, clarity and much joy.

PART 1
CREATING YOUR PRACTICE

CHAPTER 1: START WHERE YOU ARE

WHAT I SHARE IN THIS workbook comes from decades of learning to work with the different guides who showed up when I quieted my mind. My intention with this workbook is to give you the tools you need, including proven scripts and tips, to work with your spirit guides starting right where you are today. We all have access to inner wisdom from our soul and guides. There are no tests to pass and no gatekeepers to the wisdom and love they share.

BUSTING MYTHS

BEFORE YOU START, LET'S BUST some myths about working with guides.

- It doesn't require a quiet space. We learn the practices best in a private place, but that's not a requirement.
- You don't need big chunks of uninterrupted time.
- You don't have to reach some level of "goodness" before you can work with your guides. You're worthy, just as you are, of all their love and support.
- You don't need to know the names of your guides or who they are.
- You don't need to see, feel, or hear your guides—ever—to work with them. You just need to pay attention and notice what happens.
- No special equipment is needed. The guides don't care, they just want to help.

If you're willing to try out the new approaches proposed in this workbook, you will find that you can easily work with your spirit guides using the processes, tools, and scripts provided.

QUICK CHECK-IN: WHERE YOU ARE RIGHT NOW

SINCE WE'RE STARTING WHERE YOU are now, let's figure out where that is. Here's a brief list of three questions for you to answer to see how you're feeling about working with your guides. It's important to note that this is just to gauge how you feel right now, not to judge yourself or the process. We'll check in again in the middle and at the end of the workbook to see how things have improved and demonstrate your progress.

Using a range of one to five, with one being the lowest and five being the highest, answer these questions, writing in the number in the space provided:

- Do you know how to work with your guides?

....

- Do you know what guidance looks like and how to tell if you're getting it?

....

- Do you feel confident that you can tell the difference between guidance and just making something up?

....

Another way you'll measure your progress is by creating a clear image of yourself and how you'll feel once you're able to work with your guides and trust the answers you're getting. Let's imagine this future vision of you: calm, confident, clear, and creating what you want.

It's helpful to have a vision of where you want to get to, and who you'll be once you're there, to drive toward. How do you feel, how does your day go when you're able to work with your guides? How does it feel to know you have support all around you? What happens when you're clear on what to do next to get what you want? How does feeling calm change your days?

Use the following blank space to draw, paint, scribble notes, paste photos, and/or use stickers to describe your vision of how you'll feel and who you'll be when you're working with your guides.

GETTING GUIDANCE

NOTICING AND RELEASING YOUR OLD assumptions and rigid ideas about whether you can do this and how it should work will propel you forward. This isn't a one-and-done thing. It takes time, energy, intention, and focus to create a relationship with your guides that allows you to ask for and receive guidance, but this is the same with any deep friendship or relationship. You can start right now by saying, "Hi, spirit guides of highest light, I'm looking forward to working with you. Thanks in advance for the help."

They will come closer with hugs and love and help you in every step you take while using this workbook.

It's important to remember that guidance is subtle; you have to pay attention, especially at the beginning. Here's a short list of ways guidance comes for me and my students and might show up for you:

- Goose bumps, pressure in your shoulder blades, or warmth in your heart
- A song or dream repeating, providing the answer to a question
- A feeling of optimism, joy, or love washing over you for no apparent reason
- Via external messages, like hearing answers you're seeking in others' conversations, or seeing objects (such as billboards or license plates) that relate to a question or concern you have.

Do any of these apply to you, or do you have ideas about other ways the guides work with you?

....

....

....

....

....

....

....

....

....

....

....

....

HOW THIS WORKBOOK IS ORGANIZED

WE'LL START WITH HOW GUIDANCE comes (and how you're already perceiving it in subtle ways), how to set up a practice where you can trust what you're sensing, types of guides, how to ask for help, and how to work with your guides to reach your dreams and goals. Then we'll pull it all together into a sustainable practice that fits into your life—all with quick tips and scripts along the way so you can start working with your guides from this first chapter.

Knowing you can trust your guides is key to getting great guidance. Giving your trust to just any guide isn't the best way to get started, though. You want quality guidance that's for your highest good. By the end of this workbook, you'll have all the tools you need to work with your spirit guides and trust their guidance. We'll look at the tools and basic framework for communicating with them in Chapter 2.

CHAPTER 2: TOOLS YOU'LL USE

Nothing fancy needed here, the only physical tools you'll use are:

- A pen and notebook, and/or
- A place to take notes or record thoughts in your phone or computer, and/or
- This workbook

MIND AND BODY TOOLS

In addition to the physical tools, we'll apply three aspects of your mind and body to help you work with your guides:

- Intention,
- Imagination, and
- Energy, or inspired action.

INTENTION

Using your intention focuses your mind and spirit on what you want. Why does this matter? You could leave these intentions out and just start asking for guidance, but don't you want guidance that gives you the best help? That is loving, gentle, and comforting? That gives you confidence in what you're sensing and in any actions you take because of that guidance? Of course you do.

TRY THIS

Here's a quick script you can say now.

"I intend to be surrounded and supported only by my guides of the highest love and light as I read or listen to *Spirit Guides on Speed Dial* and work through these processes. I intend to learn to communicate with my guides in a way that is filled with ease, love, and joy. I am grateful for the support. So be it."

Revise this script as feels best for you.

IMAGINATION

LOOK AT ALL THE WAYS you can use your imagination as you go through your day. If we start with the assumption that your guides are all around you, you can imagine that help is always at hand when you're looking for a parking space, or when you sit down to create.

TRY THIS

Let's do an imagination check-in.

- What images or possibilities popped into your head as you read or listened to the message from my guides in *Spirit Guides on Speed Dial*?

....

....

....

....

....

- How do you currently use your imagination to go after what you want?

....

....

....

....

....

- Does your imagination kick in when you listen to audiobooks or podcasts? Or are you more inspired by images (in decorating, gardening, or cooking magazines, for instance)?

....

....

....

....

....

....

....

- Is there some time in your past when you stopped using your imagination, maybe due to something someone told you about being an adult or it being a waste of time?

....

....

....

....

....

....

....

- Draw, sketch, write or paste images of how you imagine joyfully working with your guides.

ENERGY

ENERGY RELATES TO YOUR COMMITMENT, focus, and action when you feel nudged to do something. Since guidance comes in myriad ways and can be gentle and still, your focus is on paying attention. Learning to act on what you perceive takes trust in yourself and your guides, and you'll develop that as you work with them.

Your body can be an important partner in using your energy to receive guidance. Your body is on the front line of perceiving guidance, so you might already be aware of how it helps you apply what you're learning in this workbook. Moving your body can help you receive guidance as well.

Sometimes it helps to grease the wheels a bit and do some movement before meditating to make it easier for your body to adjust to higher frequencies. You could do some easy stretches or yoga for a few minutes, or dance to music that puts you in a contemplative mood or opens your heart.

Movement during your meditations or interactions with your guides can support the experience; it helps you go beyond the monkey mind and get inspired. I find that I frequently get great guidance while walking. Some of my students have noticed this happens when they run or work out.

It may be that you're guided to move during interactions with your guides even if you've been sitting quietly, trying to get answers. Pay attention to your body: it might want to move, dance, or assume a pose.

Your body is the last energetic system to assimilate the energies of your meditation. You are accessing higher frequencies even as you start to ask for guidance. See if you feel like moving after meditation. Get in touch with what your body wants, and you may find that clarity or comfort flows in.

TRY THIS

What movement do you enjoy, what works for you?

....

....

....

....

How might you incorporate movement into getting messages? What does your body prompt you to do that allows you to receive with ease and joyful grace?

....

....

....

....

I love to ask a question and then take a walk or clean a closet, letting go of the question. Something frequently pops up in my head as I'm doing something else. Try this to see if it works for you.

....

....

....

....

CHAPTER 3: HOW YOU RECEIVE GUIDANCE

ONCE WE GO OVER THE ways you might receive guidance, you may realize that you've already been getting it, and we can build upon that. You may also feel like you're not going to get guidance, because why would they bother with you? If that's the case, please just try. You are worthy of all good things coming to you, including love and support. We all are.

You don't have to get specific answers to questions to be bathed in love, either; it just flows from your guides because their role is to help you feel it. And you might find that it's just as good as answers to your questions.

HOW GUIDANCE SHOWS UP

YOUR GUIDES ARE ALWAYS WITH you, ready to help, so we're just starting the conversation and helping to move it along. The guidance comes as nudges, intuitions, hunches. It can be very subtle—more like hints than hits on the head.

You don't have to be good at visualization or meditation for this to work. How does this inner voice, this guidance, show up for you? For me, it's a very quiet, gentle voice that usually asks a question about doing something differently—or it's a bad feeling in my stomach or my heart that something's wrong and I need to pay attention right now. Our bodies carry a lot of wisdom, so think of how guidance might feel as well as how it might show up in your thoughts.

In Chapter 1 of *Spirit Guides on Speed Dial*, I mentioned some of the ways that guidance comes for me and my students. Here is a more comprehensive list of how you might experience it.

- You get goose bumps when angels or other guides are around. Many people do. It happens to me sometimes when I'm talking to someone, which tells me that a message for them may be coming in.
- You feel pressure in your shoulder blades, where your wings would be if you had them.
- You feel nervous excitement in your stomach.
- You feel a pleasant warmth in your heart (nothing scary or heart palpitations).
- You suddenly feel expansive, positive, or filled with light (this is hard to describe!).
- You wake up with a song going through your head, and the lyrics relate to something you're wondering about (this happens to me a lot).
- Someone important to you, famous or a mentor, comes to you in a dream. You might get a direct message from this person, or their presence might be part of a message.
- You keep seeing the same numbers, 12:12 on a clock, for instance, and find that what you're doing at those moments is important. The appearance of these numbers can also mean that your guides are with you.
- You overhear a conversation—while waiting in line for a coffee or lunch, for example—that answers a specific question you've had.
- Books fall off shelves in front of you, or you remember a book you'd forgotten you have and find it quickly.
- You consistently smell perfume, roses, or some other scent. This can indicate the presence of a specific guide or an ancestor. For a decade or so after the birth of my children, my father showed up from time to time. With him, it was the smell of cigarettes (no one I know smokes, but he did so it was obvious).
- Emails or online notifications come up for something you've really wanted without you having to look for it. I've enrolled in several

courses this way or learned about someone with the expertise I'm looking for.

- You notice that people around you are talking about something you've wanted to do but haven't, and they weren't interested in that thing before. This happened to me with painting after my divorce: suddenly, multiple people in my life were interested in learning to paint and just kept talking about it. I'd been feeling the urge to do it myself, but I'd never studied and didn't know how to start. Once I finally got some paints and canvases, none of them ever mentioned painting again. I learned great lessons of surrender in the painting process that helped me work with my guides more deeply.

- You feel a strong resonance in your heart and body when in the presence of what feels like truth. When I read about a course I should take or recognize a dream I should follow, it makes me cry or takes my breath away and I feel an immediate need for it. It's almost like my spine lines up, clicks into place like a row of LEGOs.

Which of these already applies to you? How did you find this workbook? Your guides helped get you here, so look at how that happened.

THE BASIC STEPS

THE BEST WAY TO START talking to your guides is whatever comes from your heart and feels comfortable to do. Just start the basic conversation with a welcome, how you'd say hi to someone you'd like to be friends with. You're simply setting the intention and saying hi. We'll keep adding details as you read through the workbook or listen to it, but this starts the process and lets your guides know that you're ready to receive more.

There are four small steps to getting started.

- Take three deep breaths.
- Get grounded.
- Create a safe space.
- Set your intention to get great support.

Take three deep breaths.

You won't always need to do this, but it's good to get into the habit as it's the number one thing you can use to quickly calm yourself down and it can be done anywhere. Take a deep breath, one that fills up your belly. Hold it for a count of three or so, let it out slowly (or puff it out loudly if you're tense or upset; the puffing seems to carry negative energy out of your body), rest for a count of three, and then repeat the process two more times. I find that by the end of the third breath, my head feels clearer, and my body feels calmer.

This is the breathing process I use, and it works for me, but an early reader pointed me to the book *Breath* by James Nestor and the breathing exercises noted there. If you already use deep breathing techniques, or if you find a practice such as those shared in *Breath* that brings you clarity and a feeling of calm peace in your body, go ahead and substitute that for what I described.

Try this now, note what worked.

....

....

....

....

....

....

....

....

....

....

....

....

....

....

....

....

Get grounded.

There are many ways to try, but here's one that works well for many of my students: Stand up and imagine that you're a tree and roots are coming out of your feet, into the earth, going down at least three feet into the soil. Feel how that both anchors and centers you.

Another way is to imagine there are magnets on the soles of your feet pulling you to the earth (a bit too mechanical for me, but it might work great for you). Playing with modeling clay is grounding, too, or putting your hands into the soil around a house plant. It's all about your connection to the planet, so this is part of the reason putting your bare feet on the ground or on a sandy beach feels so good.

Try this now, note what worked.

....

....

....

....

....

....

....

....

....

....

Create a safe space.

This means making sure that you're someplace where you feel physically safe and free of distractions while you focus inward or close your eyes. It also means ensuring that you are protected from negative energies and only call upon guides of the highest light.

It's easy to stop interactions with any energies that don't feel right when you first start to reach out for guidance. You clearly state, "I set the intention to be surrounded and supported by only my guides of highest light. I call upon these guides to clear my energetic space of all lower energies now."

Try this, revise the script as feels best, note how it felt.

....

....

....

....

....

....

....

....

....

....

I've included scripts at the end of this chapter to help with this.

Set your intention to receive great guidance.

Set an intention to receive guidance in an easy and recognizable way, and it will happen. You can do this right now, just say the following: "I intend to receive clear guidance that's easy to understand and follow."

Try this now, change the text as feels best.

....

....

....

....

....

....

....

....

....

....

....

Start with the expectation that learning to sense (hear, feel, or see) your guidance will take a while. You're developing deep friendships that you can count on; these relationships always take time and can also feel joyous right from the start. No one, including me, just starts having great interactions with their guides. Like any deep friendship, it's worth the effort.

TRY THIS

You can use these simple scripts to get started. Change the wording as feels most comfortable for you and make note of it to use later. We will build upon these initial steps to create a process template for you in Chapter 6. For now, it's more important to just begin.

- Get grounded: Imagine roots growing from your feet into the ground, or magnets on the soles of your feet holding you steady on the planet.
- Create a safe space: Say, "I intend to work only with spirit guides of the highest love, and to always be in a safe space when working with my guides."
- Set your intention: "I intend to reach out to my spirit guides to get answers, and to be open to getting guidance and understanding what's being shared. I know this will be a back-and-forth process that takes time to work out. I intend for this process to feel joyful and supportive."
- Ask something. It can be something specific or general. Here are some examples:
- "I ask my guides to walk with me through my day and help me feel their presence."
- "I ask for help dealing with my grumpy coworker today."
- "I ask for help knowing how best to stay patient with my kids today."
- "I ask for help dealing with my health concerns."
- "I ask for answers to how I can find more money to get through each month."

Note what you're asking about and any changes you made to the scripts. How did this feel?

TYPES OF GUIDES AND YOUR GUIDES

IF YOU ALREADY HAVE GUIDES that you call upon and/or include in your prayers or meditations, such as saints, deities, loved ones who have passed, or spiritual teachers, keep working with them. This work will simply augment and support those relationships and practices, not take anything away from them.

If you're looking to connect with your intuition, your own soul's guidance, and don't have much interest in other kinds of guides, everything else in this workbook still applies.

The following list comes from the types of guides I've interacted with over the past thirty-five years personally and with my clients and students. None of them are specific to me or certain groups or types of people—we all get to benefit from them if we want to.

Angels. The angels provide comfort, protection, and a clear sense that you're interacting with the Divine. There are many types of angels and hierarchies you can call upon. People most frequently work with their guardian angel, healing angels, and archangels. This is a broad category of beings who provide healing, protection, and feelings of grace, joy and ease.

Goddesses, gods, saints, or deities. These guides come forward with a particular focus on helping you access their energies, skills, and powers to complete part of your work on the physical plane. As we move away from the old patriarchal energies of punitive power and into a more equitable age, I anticipate that more of these entities will come forward to support us. Many of them were suppressed as part of limitations imposed on our abilities to access our true worth and power or turned into mythological figures known only through stories.

Star beings (you might think of these as aliens). You may feel you're from another place in the cosmos or are looking for innovative ways to solve problems in society. The star beings bring new energy technologies and wisdom teachings from planetary cultures much older than Earth. We all have these connections, and you can go down a rabbit hole trying to figure them out. It can be easiest to start by asking for help finding innovative solutions to your concerns, as they are great at this. You can also ask for assistance in line with your soul lineage. Some star beings you may have heard of are the Andromedans, Arcturians, and Sirians. My work, especially the work I do to anchor light on the planet, increasingly involves partnering with star beings.

Ascended masters. The ascended masters have significant teachings to share on energy technologies, healing modalities, spiritual growth, embodying your soul essence, and increasing your resonance in support of your divine mission. If the word "masters" is offensive, they can be referred to as enlightened beings, ones who achieved spiritual expertise that they now share with us. Many people will partner with a specific enlightened being for much of their spiritual work, and there are many online resources that provide additional details about these guides. I generally work with them on specific concerns for shorter periods of time.

Ancestors. In many cases, ancestor spirits are not linked to your birth family. They come forward from past lives on this planet and others and can have links to current cultures or global issues. For instance, many people involved in work to support the Earth may have Indigenous elders or shamans as guides who can share their wisdom about living in harmony with the planet. Although I don't have shamanic training in this life, I have shamanic ancestors, both

29

male and female, who work with me. It's important to maintain spiritual integrity around this and not claim expertise—such as calling yourself a shaman—if you haven't trained with traditional shamanic practitioners. As you develop your spiritual practice, you'll notice that people sometimes claim this kind of knowledge or share their ideas of wisdom teachings from ancestors without true experience. Discernment is part of your spiritual path.

Nature spirits. Nature spirits can be particularly helpful if you want a stronger connection to the planet and/or are interested in supporting environmental healing. A key aspect of my energy work is forging new relationships with nature spirits and the elemental kingdom. These guides will be increasingly critical to figuring out how to live more sustainably on the planet, and part of our role as spiritually oriented humans can be to work with these beings to preserve the planet.

Higher self. Your higher self is the part of you that isn't confined to this 3D reality, it is the expanded, wiser, higher-dimensional aspects of your soul. A huge part of our mission in this life involves accessing and embodying more aspects of our higher self, which exists in an expanded state unconstrained by the human body. As we work with our guides, our ability to access our higher self through our intuition and dreams increases. In fact, many people who begin working with a spiritual guide come to realize that it is, in fact, their higher self. All the practices in this workbook can be used to increase your intuition and your connection to your higher self.

What are your thoughts on this list? Have you heard about all of these guides? If not, which ones are you most curious about or interested in? How would you like to work with these guides?

GOOD SPIRITUAL MANNERS

THERE ARE SEVERAL THINGS TO understand about working with your guides that aren't requirements but will create a solid framework for your communications.

- Treat your guides with respect, as you would any close friends. If you ask them for help, try to sense their guidance. If you don't sense anything, ask them to help you perceive them and for their guidance to be easy to understand. If you do sense something, let them know so they can build upon what's working.
- If you set up a standing time when you will be asking for guidance, say before bed, show up. If you're not sure you can stay with a set time, don't set up that expectation for you or for them. (I'm not good at sticking to a specific time, so I don't set things up that way.) You can always change or revise the expectation but do try to honor your intention.
- Don't ask the guides to do things for or to other people—this work is only for you. In Chapter 8, I will share guidance on how to ask for support for someone in a way that doesn't violate their free will and is for the highest good of all.
- Guidance will never be angry or negative. Ever. In fact, that's one of the best ways to check whether you're making something up: if a message is judgmental, peevish, irritated, or angry, it's not coming from the guides. Please bring a similarly positive energy to them. If you're going through a crisis, it's okay to be agitated and even angry—I've been that way too—but try and dial it back as much as possible. They are always here to help.
- Be grateful for their presence and support, even as you're learning to perceive and understand it.

What are your thoughts reading this? Does it seem like something you would incorporate into your practice, or something similar?

....

....

....

....

....

....

GRATITUDE

CREATING A SIMPLE GRATITUDE PRACTICE is also a great way to start receiving guidance, since your higher self and guides can come closer to you when your heart is open. Expressing your gratitude is the easiest way to receive regular guidance.

How can you incorporate a gratitude practice into your work with your guides? Do you already have a similar practice?

....

....

....

....

....

....

TRY THIS

Are you drawn to a particular type of guide?

....

....

....

....

Do you already have a prayer practice that includes one or more of the guides I listed?

....

....

....

....

Is there a kind of guide you've always wanted to work with, like an angel or goddess? Ask for their input directly or ask about an issue related to the kind of help they provide.

....

....

....

....

Have you sensed the presence of any of these guides before, or wondered about specific guides based on things you've read or seen in movies or online? If so, welcome their input on how you can work with them.

....

....

....

....

Here are some sample questions to use to start the conversation. Note any thoughts or feelings you have related to these questions in the space following this list.

- Why am I drawn to this workbook and working with you now?
- I've always wanted to feel the presence of angels (or substitute from the list)—why is that?
- Can you show me a sign that you are with me?
- How would you like to work with me?
- Is there a best way to start feeling your comfort and guidance?

What do these questions bring up? Did you try any? What happened?

....

....

....

....

....

....

....

....

....

I think these questions are perfect for walking meditations, especially in a beautiful park or other setting where there's a bit of wild nature to get your thoughts and feelings flowing.

You can also just say, "I want more guidance; I'm open to getting more guidance."

Ask for help. This is a huge deal—just ask. Talk to them; they hear you. Just notice things and then ask for help figuring out what they mean. Ask for help a lot. Be grateful and ask for help! That pretty much takes care of all of it. Now you know how to start having a solid relationship with your guides.

....

....

....

....

Try this, note how it felt.

....

....

....

....
....
....
....
....
....
....
....
....
....
....

After you've opened the conversation with your question or questions, pay close attention to your thoughts and what appears in front of you over the next few days. Remember, guidance can show up in many ways.

This was a big chapter. We went over a lot of things that might be very new to you. This prep work is critical; you're starting to work with your tools and assembling the pieces of the practice you'll create in the coming chapters. If you're having trouble getting your inner dialogue (or diatribes) to quiet down so you can sense guidance and your intuition, don't worry—we'll cover that in Chapter 6. For now, let's explore some of the ways your guides can help make your dreams come true, some of the best ways of working with them.

CHAPTER 4: DREAMS AND INSPIRATION

THERE ARE MULTIPLE WAYS TO go about fulfilling your dreams with the help of your guides. One is to get help pursuing a dream you already have. Another is to spend quiet time with your imagination and see what comes up as inspiration for new dreams. Big dreams, little ones, business-related dreams, even finding the perfect recipe to help create a family holiday tradition—it doesn't matter. You can call in guides to help with the specifics without knowing their names or what kinds of guides they are; you just ask for the help you need and make sure to ask that it be easy and joyful at the same time. Getting help to dream big should be fun and freeing.

What if you're not sure what your dreams are? You can ask for help remembering dreams you buried, or expanding on what you think might be possible. Movies or books might be good inspirations in this instance: is there a theme among the stories you love? Look for the hints in your life.

Walking meditation is great for entering a dream state that moves past mental ideas of what's possible, as is journaling. Using visuals from magazines or social media feeds can inspire new visions of what you'd love to create or experience. There are some great books on using your imagination and staying playful included in the recommended resources on my website at Julesapollo.com/extras. The point of working with the guides is to move beyond what you think and into the power of bigger possibilities that come through your heart and connection to your guides and your expanded self.

WHAT IF YOU CAN'T IMAGINE ANY DREAMS?

IF YOU'RE IN A TRAUMATIC time or struggling to get by, you may not be able to articulate exactly what you'd like to be different or how things would be if they were ideal. Maybe you struggle to imagine how you'd feel if things were better. The guides can help with this, as well as give you glimpses of your greater potential and possibilities. Here's a script to start with.

"I call upon all my guides of highest light and love and my higher self. I'm having trouble imagining what my dreams are, how things could get better, and how I might feel once they are. Please help me sense what's possible for me that I can't see now. Please bring me images and inspiration for better times, ways I can be more at ease, and ways I can see and experience more of my potential. Please bring all of this with ease, grace, flow, and joy. Hold me in your light and love and help me release anything that holds me back from imagining and realizing my dreams and my full potential. I am so grateful for your help. Thank you."

Try this now, change the wording as fits you.

ASKING FOR HELP

LIKE ANYTHING ELSE YOU'RE WORKING on or want support for, going after your dreams is something you can do with the help of your guides. Here's a simple script to use:

"I call upon all my guides of highest light and my creative muses. Please support me in making my dream come true by sharing inspiration regarding details of this dream, actions to take in support of the dream, and the energy and commitment to follow through on making this dream come true. I am open to receiving guidance on how to make this dream even better than I've imagined. I ask to be filled to the brim with inspiration and held in love while I'm dreaming. I'm grateful for the support."

Try this now, change the wording as fits you.

"WHAT IF?" AND "HOW GOOD CAN I LET IT BE?"

SOMETIMES MY DREAMS ARE CONSTRICTED by what I think is possible, what I've been told I could have, or what's happened before. This constraint is unnecessary and something the guides can help you blow past. One way to deal with it is to ask the questions "What if?" and "How good can I let it be?" I find that the answers I get to these questions are especially expansive if I ask them while doing something relaxing, like sitting in a warm bath or a beautiful garden.

Here's an example. Let's say you're looking for a new job. You could think about the kind of job you want and the place you'd like to work, then ask questions that help create what you want but also expand your ideas of what is possible.

"What if I liked my coworkers? What if I got a great raise? What if I got to use all my skills? What if my boss and the teams I worked with recognized and respected my skills and experience? What if I had flexible hours or could work at home? What if I worked someplace where I could take a walk in a park at lunch? What if there were great opportunities for me to advance in the company?"

Note any thoughts you have here: how can you use this in your life and dreams right now?

....

....

....

....

....

....

You can do this with anything you dream about: having more money to pay bills, resolving your health issues, finding the perfect partner, living in a great place, etc.

The same goes for "How good can I let it be?" Let's say you have dreams of starting a business so you don't need to work for anyone else, and you're thinking about what that could be. You consider the skills you have and what you could offer that people might want—but do you think of what would bring you the greatest joy? What could you create that would bring you not only financial freedom but also the kind of wealth that gives you sovereignty in life and complete freedom in *all* your decisions?

Note any thoughts you have here: how can you use this in your life and dreams right now?

....

....

....

....

....

....

....

....

....

....

....

Don't stop reading now just because you think that will never be possible. Imagine—that's all we're doing here. What if you could be sovereign in your life, making decisions with a focus on joy and freedom? What would that feel like? Again, just dream and expand what you imagine might be possible. Try on what that would feel like and how you'd move through your day if it was your reality, and then make it even better. How yummy can you let it feel when your dreams come true? Of course, ask your guides to help you with this; that's the whole point of this chapter. Play with these questions and approaches to see if what you're imagining can get even better. Your soul might want things that your mind never thought you could obtain.

Note any thoughts you have here: how can you use this in your life and dreams right now?

....

....

....

....

....

....

....

....

....

....

....

....

Making sure I'm not limiting how much joy I feel is a big part of dreaming. Feeling bliss is part of the way I feel free. Bliss to me is a subversive emotion, a stealthy way of breaking the paradigm of economic suppression and burden that so many people feel on this planet. Thinking of myself as a spiritual rebel, busting the dominant, suppressive paradigm with my dreaming, makes it even more fun for me.

As we become more heart-centered, we become better able to envision, create, and empower our lives. We can call in our power and create the world of our dreams. We are experts at this; we create our reality and the world we live in through our thoughts and actions every day. We're just not used to thinking of it that way.

TRY THIS

Here's an easy script to use to ask your guides for inspiration and to help you make your dreams come true. You can start with a specific dream, like a vacation, or a broader dream like starting your own business while you're still figuring out exact details to focus on.

"I am dreaming of (whatever), and I ask my guides to help me make it real. I ask for guidance related to specific steps, and for help in imagining what might be even better than I've thought possible. If this dream is

not for my highest good, please give me gentle nudges toward what is better. I ask to be cocooned in a dreaming state in the comfort of your presence. Thank you."

Revise this to fit you or note your thoughts.

Here are some ideas for jump-starting your imagination and dreaming.

- Take a vision vacation in a peaceful place (imagined or real), adding in as many details of the completed dream or vision as possible. Use your senses to fill in details to help it feel complete: what are you smelling, seeing, tasting, feeling when your dream's real?
- Do the "What if?" and "How good can I let it be?" exercises for expansive possibilities.
- Fill your creative well with art, music, or movies. Bring your guides along. This concept of an "Artist Date" comes from Julia Cameron's book *The Artist's Way*. I try to do this once a week, even if it's just spending time looking at images or videos. To me, that's a beauty break and it helps replenish me.
- Keep a journal by your bed and track your dreams. Write down a question or something you'd like guidance on before you go to sleep and any dreams you remember when you wake up.

Which of these might work for you, and how can you fit them in to your dreaming? Make notes below, color, use stickers, mind map, or paste images.

....

....

....

....

....

....

....

Can you see how the tools we've gone over so far will support you in trusting the guidance you receive and getting help with your dreams? Once you move past the initial dreaming stage and start taking action inspired by your dreams, you're ready to work with your guides to accomplish your goals. That's what we'll cover in the next chapter.

CHAPTER 5: GUIDES AND GOALS

ONCE YOU HAVE A WORKING process for communicating with your guides, you can use their help to reach your goals in both general and specific ways, even if you don't have a strong sense of their presence. Think of them as a support system that gives you both a framework for decision-making and details on how to complete individual tasks that will help you realize your vision.

Your guides can support and amplify your efforts and help you decide on the next steps or best choices, but the decision to do something, and the actions required to move forward with what you want, come from you. Your guides help sustain the effort and bolster your confidence in your ability to complete it. That is where your partnership really kicks in.

There are a lot of similarities between how you go about this and how you get general support for your dreams, but the difference here is setting an intention and carrying out the actions. All the tools discussed earlier—intention, imagination, and energy—apply here with additional focused energy because you have a targeted intention. This is where you can best apply the whole toolkit shared in this workbook to identify what you need, to ask for what you specifically need help with, and to let the guides figure out how to get it done.

You can ask the guides to help you be efficient with your time and how you approach defining the goal: breaking it down into steps, revising as you go along, and prioritizing the work. You can also ask specifically for guides of efficiency and those with the energy to jump in and help; you don't need to know their specific names or types.

You're doing the work you'd usually do to accomplish something but asking for support and inspiration along the way, so you get into a flow of ideas and action more easily and are energetically supported by the guides as you're doing it.

You can apply the same approach to big goals related to health, wealth, or love, and to targeted goals such as updating a page on your website or designing and planting a peaceful garden—even tiny things like quickly getting in and out of the DMV when you renew your driver's license. In fact, turning something that's usually painful (like renewing a driver's license) into an easy—dare I say fun—exercise brings me great joy. I feel triumphant when these little victories happen, and ready to look for more ways to make situations easier.

One of the miracles of this work is that it provides you with so much more time to pursue your goals. You might set an intention to prepare for efficient interactions with agencies or banks, for instance, to remove the stress and time usually needed for mundane activities. This can feel so magical and playful that it makes me laugh, and it's another way I know my guides are around, even when I don't sense them.

Here are some examples of things the guides can help bring to you:

- Mentors
- Programs or new teachings so you can gain necessary skills
- Innovative ideas
- New collaborative partners
- Money or time to pursue your goals
- Access to specialists and experts
- Revelations of limiting beliefs that are blocking your success
- Visions of how to complete your goals
- Synchronicities of all kinds, like meeting people or hearing about opportunities.

When I teach a class or work with clients one-on-one, their experiences convince them that working with their guides to reach their goals is bringing them concrete results. Examples they have shared with me include:

- Finding not only mentorship programs, but also paid mentorships offered by the exact program they wanted but didn't think they could get into
- New approaches and experts coming to help with a family member's critical health issues
- Being introduced by friends to people who become collaborative partners in new business or creative endeavors
- Finally enjoying success with dating after divorce
- Having ideas for a new fiction series come through dreams after a creative drought that had them doubting their ability to continue writing.

When they started working with me, these students and clients didn't imagine that such successes were even possible. We dug up their dreams, worked on developing their goals, and then created steps they could take to ask for help from the guides, watch for signs, and act on the guidance and opportunities that seemed to drop into their laps. You now have the tools that will allow similar surprises to show up in your life.

TRY THIS

As you read or heard me read the list above, what popped in your head? How might you call in support for goals you're already pursuing? How could you ask for help to decide the best course of action if you're undecided about what to do next?

....

....

....

....

....
....
....
....
....
....

Here's an example script:

"I call upon all my guides who can help me break down my goals into actionable steps and be efficient with my energy and time so I can succeed in reaching my goals with ease, grace, flow, and joy. I ask for support in noticing the ways I block my flow, and guidance to joyfully create the success I seek. I'm deeply grateful for the help."

Revise or add to this as best for you.

....
....
....
....
....
....
....
....

THE GODDESS GUIDE TO GOAL SETTING

I HAVE A GODDESS COUNCIL that includes a variety of goddesses I can call upon, depending on what's going on. The Goddess Isis is one of my main guides, and she is always present when I'm trying to create something.

Here's how I like to explain working with the goddesses: Archangel Michael is the sky, vast and powerful. The Goddess Isis folds the sky into a laser and asks what you want to do with it. Goddesses bring the power of that laser to your goal. They help me target what I want and where I want to go, and they come in full-on with how to get it done.

The goddesses gave me a concise framework for completing goals with their support: envision, empower, anchor, and act. Here's how it works for me:

Envision. This is the dreaming part, using your imagination in as much detail as you can. How does this goal look when it is complete, and how will you feel? What is the specific outcome you're looking for? Imagine as many of the sensory details as possible, especially related to how you'll feel when you've reached your goal. The specific details can and probably will change as you pursue it, but it's the feeling, the resonance of that realized goal that you're aiming for.

Empower. Call in your guides, all the support you need. This isn't a one-and-done request, but it's the next step because it allows you to start and continue to pursue your goals in partnership with them and their energy, power, and wisdom.

Anchor. This is your intention. You anchor yourself to the earth and then anchor your intention to go after and complete your goal. It's important to get grounded and state your goal out loud. If it helps, you can stand up and assume a Wonder Woman pose (hands on hips, confidently declaring what you intend to do).

Act. This is the step of applying your energy to take inspired action, and it can trip us up because we struggle to understand what is inspired versus what we think we should do. So, ask for help identifying your next *inspired* action. I always go back to what feels joyful. An action might feel intimidating or like it's a bit too much, but if it makes you feel excited, even gleeful, that's inspired. Think of how little kids play with complete abandon—we want to bring a similar energy to the pursuit of our dreams and goals.

Tara Mohr, author of the book *Playing Big* and creator of a great program of the same name, talks about two different kinds of fear. The first is the fear we feel when we imagine what could go wrong (often invented and improbable) that makes us shrink away from doing or trying something. We feel the second kind of fear when we're expanding, occupying more space than we're used to. This fear is called *yirah* in Hebrew, and it can feel exciting at the same time. We're aiming for the feeling of *yirah* in our goals and inspired actions. Remember "How good can you let it be?" Links to Tara's book and program are included on the resource page of my website: https://julesapollo.com/extras.)

Again, this isn't a one-and-done kind of process. You might go through it and change some of the details or even your goal after you take action. I'd be surprised if you didn't.

You can do the four steps quickly. After your envisioning stage, you can set up a goals council and call them in, just as you'd set up a meeting at work. How do you do this? You just call them in. If there's a specific being you'd like to have support from, call them in. If you don't have a specific guide you'd like to work with, you can ask for guides related to helping you succeed at completing your goal. Don't worry, there's a script for this shared in the coming paragraphs.

One of the most joyful ways for me to create is in community with my guides. It's playful and empowering at the same time. Who do you want on your goal council? You could start by saying something like:

"I'm calling forth all my guides of highest light who can support me in reaching my goal of (whatever you want, starting a business, for example). Please bring me inspiration and support and help me envision the best possible result I can create, discern what actions I should take and what I can leave to you, and make the process exciting and fun. I call forth the energy of (specific guide or archetypal energy of creative mastery, for instance, if you have someone in mind). Please make your guidance clear and easy to understand. I'm so grateful for the support. Thank you."

What are your thoughts reading through the steps? Change the script to best fit you and note any thoughts on the process and how it might work for you.

....

....

....

....

....

....

....

....

....

....

....

There are many beings of light around the planet now, providing energy and innovative ideas at this time of the collapse of old power systems. Use your particular skills and interests to call in guides that can help you make an impact as well. Creating a healthy, just, peaceful planet is going to take all of us.

TRY THIS

What skills do you have that could be applied to create a more just world and healthy planet? What brings you great joy that you could use, in work with your guides, to anchor more light and spread more love around? Do you have technical expertise that could be applied in partnership with your guides to create a better world?

....

....

....

....

....

....

....

....

....

....

....

....

....

....

Everything helps, and all your love is needed now. It's time to play with the light that you and your guides bring. Just moving through your day surrounded by the love you've called in, with an open heart, helps a great deal and keeps your energy high.

After all this talk about dreams, goals, and the tools you can use to work with your guides, I hope you feel ready to dive into the deep end and create a practice that fits your life. Great timing, as that's just what we'll do in Chapter 6.

CHAPTER 6: CREATING YOUR PRACTICE

THE POINT OF THIS CHAPTER is to pull together the pieces we've already discussed and create a quick template, with scripts, for your practice that you can adjust over time.

We're going to set up a practice that fits into your life so you have a better chance of doing it. The most important part is to make it easy. There are a few things you can do to approach your practice that way from the start.

Figure out the best time of day for you to work with your guides. Choose a time when you'll be able to focus on the process. There's no sense trying to work with them right before you go to sleep if you're always exhausted. What time of day are you most alert and efficient? Squeeze in a few minutes during that period to reach out to your guides.

What's your best time of day? How can you fit a few minutes to reach out to your guides during this time?

Stay open to being guided, moved, or inspired. I read once that Oprah asks to be blessed into service each day—that's another way to look at being moved or inspired.

Be open to answers or what you're looking for coming in unanticipated ways. If you ask about money, be open to it coming to you through the mail, from a friend, or just showing up in your bank account. You might find it on the ground, win it as a prize, or earn it through getting new clients. You might receive an unexpected raise or bonus, or perhaps a refund will show up. You might be paid for old work or get a call out of the blue to help someone who can pay you. Guidance sometimes comes in roundabout ways that may not at first look like you're getting what you want.

You don't need to speak about all these possibilities, but you can ask for what you request to show up easily and joyfully and then let it go, trusting that your prayers and requests are heard.

Trusting the process means several things:

- Trusting your guides are around and that they will help you
- Trusting that your requests are heard and will be acted upon
- Trusting yourself to understand the guidance you receive
- Trusting yourself to take the actions you're inspired to take

You can ask your guides to help you trust. You can ask them to help you understand the guidance you get. And you can keep asking for clarity and comfort to be part of all your interactions with your guides. Being able to trust the guides and yourself is a huge part of working with them, so note anywhere you feel resistance or doubt when you read or hear the list above. Making requests for what you want and adding "or something better" can help you surrender to the way your request shows up.

How are you feeling about trusting yourself and the guides? What can you do to feel most trusting of the process, either now or setting up ways to create trust as you start working with them?

SETTING EXPECTATIONS

IT'S USUAL TO FEEL A bit nervous and insecure when you think about starting to reach out to your guides: "Will I do it right? Do I really have guides? Will they want to work with me? Have I made any mistakes in my life so bad that they won't work with me?"

Let's be clear on all of these: there's no wrong way to do this, you have many guides, and they will always work with you, no matter what. But it can take a while for you to start sensing them—or just to trust that they are with you whether you sense anything or not. Partly it's them figuring out how to communicate with you in ways you'll notice. This is why I keep mentioning that guidance can be subtle. Just note what comes up in both your internal and external lives.

Even though your guides are with you, you won't necessarily sense their physical presence. In fact, most of us don't.

If you can start your practice letting it feel natural (like you assume the lights will turn on when you flip a switch), resting in the assurance that you have loving support ready to help, and suspending any need to define how you get that support, you'll find the process more joyful, surprising, and comforting.

SCRIPTS TO HELP YOU BEGIN

HERE ARE SOME SCRIPTS TO help you get started. You can use these words to start and then revise them to fit you and your guides over time. The point is to just begin. Imagine me right next to you, holding a space for you to feel ready to create your own approach to working with your guides. All of this is flexible and meant to support, not inhibit, you. Here are the scripts, broken into the steps of beginning, request, clarity, and gratitude.

There are lines following each script to change it as you feel best works for you. Play with these steps and scripts—make them your own. All of this can be changed. It's great when it works and flows all in and around you. If you don't sense anything immediately after you make your request, go on with your day and come back later.

Beginning.

- "I set the intention that I am in a safe space while I talk with my guides, and I invoke the presence and protection of my guides of highest love to create that safe space."

....

....

....

....

....

....

....

- "I intend to be grounded and centered, with a still, calm mind, so I may best perceive the presence of my guides and the information they have to share with me."

....

....

....

....

....

....

- "I intend to work with only those guides of highest light and love, and I call forth all my guides who meet those criteria to support me now."

....

....

....

....

....

....

Request.

- "I ask that the guidance I receive be clear and easily understood. I ask for support in understanding the guidance and having clarity on the next steps and actions that best support my highest and best good now."

....

....

....

....

....

....

- Use what applies in the following list or something similar to ask for what you need.
  - "I'm asking for help with..."
  - "I'd like to get guidance related to..."
  - "I'm asking for a clear sign that you are with me."
  - "Please bring me inspiration and clarity on next steps, I'd love to create…"
  - "Please give me strength and commitment to reach my goal, I've felt like stopping…"
  - "I have a big dream; please help me hold a clear vision of how to make this come true…"

Clarity.

- "Can you share more details about this?"

....

....

....

....

....

- "Am I perceiving correctly? Please help me clearly understand."

....

....

....

....

- "I'd love to receive guidance and support on how to start making something happen."

....

....

....

....

....

Gratitude.

- "I trust that the guidance I am getting, either now or in the future in response to this request, is in support of my intention and for my highest good. Thank you all. I'm grateful. So be it and so it is."

....

....

....

....

....

TRY THIS

Play with these steps and scripts—make them your own. All of this can be changed. It's great when it works and flows all in and around you. If you don't sense anything immediately after you make your request, go on with your day and come back later.

QUIETING INNER CRITICS

YOUR INNER CRITICS MIGHT BE digging in here. In fact, you may have skimmed over the sample scripts above and decided that you're not ready and will keep reading and come back to this later. That's ok, but if it's your lizard brain jumping in, please know it's normal and there are ways to let go of things that restrict you. The key to lowering the volume of the inner critics is to lean into the support you can call on from your guides as you face the critics, question their logic, and act to release their hold on your mind and energy.

It's good to have fears and doubts come up because then you can release them with the help of your guides. This is something that might happen a lot, no matter how long you work with your guides. Any time we try to change or move into greater freedom, the inner critics marshal the troops and come calling. This happens both when we start something and as we progress. Releasing old concepts of self will always be part of your practice, so you may as well have a process in place to make it easier.

Your guides come to you in wisdom, surrounded by light and love and bathing you in these higher frequencies. Any lower-frequency energies, outdated patterns, or limiting beliefs you have will come to your attention as you work with the guides because the old energies are not in resonance with the energy you're calling forth to help you.

It's all physics: People and ideas feel good to us when they resonate with us—when they have the same vibe, you might say. As you work with your guides, you'll get comfortable with their higher frequencies. And each time you interact with them, you raise your frequency a bit to get closer to theirs. This is the concept of harmonic resonance.

It's not necessary to know the history of a pattern or revisit it to resolve it. It's not helpful to get into the energy of a pattern if it came from an abusive or damaging incident, or if it's an old family pattern. The point is to let it go. This is another place where your imagination, or a brief ritual, comes in handy.

Here are some things you could do to release old stuff as it comes up.

- Write old patterns down on a piece of paper and burn it. This can be a fun ritual to do with the moon cycles. I tend to let go of old things with the full moon and welcome new patterns or desires with the new moon. Howling is optional but freeing.
- Take a ritual bath to release an old pattern. Imagine it draining away with the water.

- Set an intention to be free of whatever's holding you back and imagine yourself in a shower of light—light that flows like water, and the old pattern is mud on your skin. Stand in this shower until the water at your feet looks clear. This is what I do at the beginning of each session with my guides in my inner sanctuary.
- Write down what your inner critics say and read it out loud. Is it logical? Would you say it to a friend? If not, tell that pattern you're no longer interested in hearing illogical thoughts and if it wants to participate in your life, it needs to be helpful or be quiet—and get your guides to support you in this. For me, this isn't a one-and-done deal, but something I use consistently. Over time, it has shut up the worst of my inner demons.
- Imagine a big bonfire and your ancestor spirits dancing around it to support you. Add some drumming or music, light some incense, and see the scene as vividly as possible as you imagine burning up whatever stinky thinking has held you back by throwing it in the fire or standing in the middle of the flames to burn it away. I stand in the flames for old family stuff.
- See each pattern like the skin of a snake and shed it if it's an old identity that no longer fits ("I don't have anything of value to share" is one I had). I imagine it as an entire skin, like a full-body mask, yank it off, and into the fire it goes.
- Plan any or all of this as part of a full moon or year-end ritual, throw in a tarot reading for the new year or cycle, and have a party with your guides. Might as well power up as part of your ritual of release. I share my favorite tarot and oracle decks here: https://julesapollo.com/extras.

TRY THIS

Pick one of these suggestions or create something that works for you in a similar way and use it on your inner critics' favorite intrusion into your day. Keep these suggestions handy for the next time you're ready to release an old pattern. Make note of which ones you might like to try here.

HOW TO FIND TIME TO TALK TO YOUR GUIDES

You may have skimmed past this whole chapter, thinking that you have no time to try any of this. You may be thinking that this is all fine and good for me, as I seem to have time to talk to my guides all the time, but you don't.

The following simple things worked for me to grab some extra time in the day. See which of these you could apply to your day.

- Do a quick check-in with your guides while your coffee is brewing.
- Run through a quick visualization or journal for a few minutes while the kids do their homework (see Chapter 5 for a reminder of how to use these tools to go after your goals with your guides).
- Leave the dishes to soak until tomorrow and call in your guides instead—
- or talk to them while you're doing dishes or loading the dishwasher. I find warm water soothing, so this is a good way for me to relax my mind and open my heart to guidance.
- Delegate or outsource something you hate. This can involve finding software to help with a task or making something you do regularly more efficient, like ordering groceries online and doing curbside pickup instead of shopping in the store. Then use the freed-up time to focus on your dreams.
- If you're waiting for a meeting to start, do some deep breathing o your mind and body aren't restricting your flow of inspiration.
- Turn off the computer early and spend that saved time to focus on goals.
- Run through the details of your goal with your guides while you're folding laundry or cooking. Cleaning is a great general way to ask your guides questions and allow answers to come while your body is doing the work.

- Figure out the times of day when you're most efficient and make working with your guides your priority at those times. Conversely, do things that can be completed without intense energy commitments during times when your energy or focus lag: for me, those things are laundry, dishes, and walking the dog. My energy tends to have revived at the end of these activities, so I get a double benefit: things are done, and I have improved focus to boot.
- Grab a few minutes before sleep to check in with your guides for inspired actions to take the next day.
- Keep a notebook by your bed and take the first ten minutes in the morning to write before anyone knows you're awake. If I wake up remembering a dream, I try and figure out what its message might be.

You need to decide that you can and will find the time you want. This is where you commit to honoring your creativity and passion. Decide that you will find a way, no matter what your family needs or what work deadlines you have, to feed your soul and free your heart by creating what wants to come out into the world.

Once you reap the benefits of a few minutes, it will be easy to find more. Think of it as a scavenger hunt. Most of these suggestions are just about using your time intentionally: what do you want to get out of your days and weeks? Make that the focus of the minutes you're grabbing.

The point of all this is to feel better about being able to get answers and support when you need it.

TRY THIS

From what's been discussed in this chapter, what pops in your head to try? Pick two things and try them out today. How did that work? Note your progress and keep going.

....

....

....

....

....

....

....

CHECK-IN

LET'S DO ANOTHER QUICK CHECK-IN like we did at the beginning of the workbook: Using a range of one to five, with one being the lowest and five being the highest, answer these questions:

- Do you know how to work with your guides?

....

- Do you know what guidance looks like and how to tell if you're getting it?

....

- Do you feel confident that you can tell the difference between guidance and just making something up?

....

Make a quick note of your numbers for each question to compare with your results from the beginning of the workbook. How do your numbers compare to the first check-in?

....

....

Look at all the new approaches you've learned and scripts you have. You've made great progress.

Let's revisit the vision you created in Chapter 1 of how you'll feel once you're able to work with your guides and trust the answers you're getting: calm, confident, clear, and creating what you want. Take a few minutes to truly see, smell, hear, feel, and imagine this as real. Is it easier to imagine this state of being now? How has your vision changed since you started the workbook? Do you feel more confident? Can you see it more clearly?

....

....

....

....

....

....

....

....

....

....

....

....

....

....

....

....

....

....

....

....

....

....

If creating an initial process to work with your guides isn't falling easily into place, the approaches in the next chapter might work. We all need help to quiet our minds so we can easily sense the guidance that's already around and being shared with us. And there are many ways to make this process work for you, no matter how chaotic your life is. I feel that the chaos in the world will only keep increasing, at least for a bit, so having ways to feel peaceful for a few minutes as you go about your day is gold. Keep going to find out how.

CHAPTER 7: HOW TO QUIET YOUR MIND IN TIMES OF CHAOS

Given how chaotic life can feel, these suggestions can probably help anyone who's feeling tense. We have to find ways to feel calm, even as we handle all the day-to-day needs and crises, or we'll never perceive the guidance we're getting.

When you're stressed and exhausted, you won't pick up on subtle nudges and you struggle to find even a few minutes to focus on guidance. In this chapter, we'll go over how to calm your mind no matter what's going on around you.

HOW TO TELL IT IT'S GUIDANCE OR YOUR MIND

I worried about this a lot when I started as I thought I might be making things up. This is a frequent concern of my students too. It's actually easy: your guides are never mean, insulting, or cross with you. The feelings they radiate are expansive, joyful, supportive, and/or comforting. While your inner critics can sometimes seem quiet, they generally tell you to do what keeps you contained and small. Listening to their critical voices can make you feel bad or lack the confidence to make big changes.

I used to double-check that I was hearing correctly, and you might want to do this as you begin to sense guidance. One way to do this is to use muscle testing, also referred to as applied kinesiology: I'm no expert at explaining this—there is plenty of information online, though, so search for a video that will show you how to do it (I tried to film one, but I have short, fat fingers so it's hard to see what I'm doing and then I kept laughing because it looked so silly). I also use tarot cards to ask questions. The main thing I still do when I'm really tense and unsure that I'm hearing correctly is stop asking, move around a bit (get a glass of water or stretch), and then ask again after making sure I'm grounded and in a safe space.

TRY THIS

Take a moment right now and think of some of your standard inner criticism. Imagine someone standing in front of you and saying these things to you or hearing someone say them to a friend or family member. They're like rude posts on social media. It's easier to see how silly they are if you expose them to the light of logic. You've outgrown them now and so you and they are ready for healing love.

Some of my inner critics are old Midwestern farm wives, like my grandmothers and great-grandmothers. "Get your work done or no play" and "You're getting too big for your britches" kind of voices. Judging and shaming are two of their favorite games. It can help to give your inner critics names or to imagine them in detail. It's easier to shut them up that way.

Here are some of the ways I've used to quiet them. My approach varies based on the voices and how nasty or debilitating they are.

- I imagine the mean grandmas on a big front porch with rockers and sweet tea, maybe some knitting. I often see them fall asleep. They didn't know times of rest, so this is a gift I can give them.
- For others who want to constrain my exuberance, who judge and shame, I take a different approach. This is one I really like: I imagine I'm at the head of a big table in an office boardroom. (Make it as fancy and sterile as you wish, that can help.) Mine is always sleek, expensive, and in a high-rise in downtown Chicago. Acting as the CEO of my life, I call the voices to the table and ask for updates. They start up their usual tripe; I stop them and

say that's old news, we've already resolved that—do you have anything new? And since most of these voices are one-trick ponies, complaining about the same thing over and over, they just look down sheepishly. I tell them that they only get to keep their seat at the table if they bring something helpful and constructive.

- I get into old loops of self-criticism. These days, I just tell those voices that it's not true what they're saying and I'm not going to listen to it. I find that some resolute firmness does the trick. I don't deserve to be treated to such tirades and neither do you.
- My main way to quiet them is to go into my inner sanctuary. There's an old, thick, medieval-looking wooden door to get into that space. I go inside and shut the door, and this keeps out everything that isn't for my highest good.
- Sometimes I surprise them by giving them a big hug, asking that they be surrounded in love. I'm usually not patient enough to do this, but it's a surefire way to silence them for a good amount of time. My most fearful critics are the ones that respond best to this. I wrap them in a bear hug, and they calm right down, like a frightened child (which the fears really are).

This is where your imagination comes in. What technique might you use?

....

....

....

....

....

....

....

....

....

....

Once you clearly hear what the inner critics are saying, an easy question to ask is if you'd say what you're hearing to a friend. If it isn't representative of the way you'd talk with someone you care about, it isn't something you need to tolerate creeping into your day and your energy.

It doesn't matter what you do to shut them up so long as you realize that these voices aren't speaking the truth, and you can move past them to get what you want. Progress comes when you keep going instead of getting stuck in their nonsense.

HOW TO QUICKLY FEEL CALMER

THE FOLLOWING SUGGESTIONS DON'T TAKE any time. You can do them as you go about your regular day. They just require some shifts: shifts in focus, in believing what you can do, in how you manage time and energy, and how you take care of yourself.

As you choose to put these practices in place, you'll move from feeling overwhelmed, discouraged, exhausted, and unappreciated at times to feeling consistently calm, relaxed, and confident that you can handle whatever life throws at you.

I've included brief breaks that take little to no time and are meant to help sustain your energy, lift your mood, or save you time. These can be sprinkled throughout your day, with the intent to help you get to the end of it feeling less stress and more energy. That way, you can squeeze in work with your guides when you have a few minutes.

I also listed some ideas for renewal rituals: ways to treat yourself once a week or so that are focused on your senses, creativity, or deep rest.

What's the result of taking these small steps? They provide fuel and sustenance so you can deal with daily life and still have time and energy to create what you want.

As you read through the list below, you'll recognize things that you're already doing, things that you already do well, and others that you can adapt to fit into your day or week right now to make things easier. Looking for solutions to what's bugging you is proactively making change, which is one of the reasons you found this workbook.

If you try nothing else, do the breathing. It can really help, and you can do it no matter what else is going on. Can't pay a bill and are panicking? Take three deep breaths. Feeling exhausted but the kids are sick? Take three deep breaths. Frozen with anxiety about the future? Three big ones and then two more sets. I sigh loudly when I breathe out if I'm worried; it seems to release the tension. This breathing practice strengthens your lungs and gets more oxygen to your body, so it's great for your overall health as well.

Here are my top suggestions for things you can try to feel calmer. Most of them take a few minutes at most.

- Take three deep belly breaths with a big sigh on the exhales.
- Check your body, breathe, and stretch to release tense muscles. Tight muscles tire you out.
- Get outside. Even a five-minute walk can help. Or listen to the sound of rain or birdsong while you work. Even photos or videos of nature can relax you a lot. YouTube videos can be great for this. I love videos of walks in different forests with the sounds of the wind in the trees and birds in the background.
- Listen to a favorite song and have a solo dance party. Music and dancing send happy hormones through the body. Make an emergency playlist for bad days and keep it handy on your phone.

This is great for loud singing in the car, too, which is another great way to release tension and feel better.

- Have a good ugly cry in the shower. I used to do this when the kids were small so they wouldn't hear me. When I finally realized how much tension and stress crying releases, I just let myself cry whenever I needed to; I didn't need a specific reason.

- Get and/or give a big, squishy hug from your kids or a dog or stuffed animal. Squishy hugs are the best!

- Close your eyes and imagine your perfect peaceful place, your inner sanctuary—someplace safe, serene, and beautiful. This is great for a commute if you're on a bus or train. (See Chapter 11 for more on creating your inner sanctuary.)

- Look into the mirror and remind yourself that you're strong, resilient, and will figure it out. Be kind to yourself and be your own cheerleader.

- Give yourself a beauty break. This is similar to the Artist Date described in Julia Cameron's *The Artist's Way*, one of my favorite books. It feeds the creative well with images or experiences. If you're crazy busy, you can squeeze a mini beauty break into your day by looking at images of art, places you want to travel, or beauty in nature on Instagram or Pinterest. Watching a movie or listening to a concert works too. I love going to the symphony or to a museum, and watching old movies is the best.

- Enjoy a relaxation ritual with a long bath, or maybe just sitting in bed with a heating pad and a journal or a good book. Let your mind wander and do nothing on your agenda or to-do list.

- Get comfy: put on pajamas and fuzzy socks, grab some pillows and a favorite treat or glass of wine, and relax.

- Take a creation break: bake, paint, color, garden, write, or build. Creating something taps the power of your mind and heart so new ideas and different perspectives can sneak in. I've found that sloppy coloring is a great way to release frustration.

Make some of the things that seem fun or easy from the list above and experiment to see what works for you.

Music is absolutely guaranteed to lift my mood and increase my energy. Put on something that you can move to with abandon or restraint, whatever suits your personality. Even a few minutes helps a lot, and you can do this while driving, unloading the dishwasher, taking out the garbage, or cleaning the bathroom. I'm old-school and created a playlist of favorites that you can find here: https://julesapollo.com/extras. Having an emergency feel-good playlist can help in times of trauma, too.

Create a playlist or a list of videos you can watch on YouTube. How can you be more playful, or build fun into your day?

RELEASING OLD FEARS AND PATTERNS

FIGURING OUT WHAT'S HOLDING YOU back and letting it go is something the guides can really help with, especially since a lot of old fears are subconscious and/or based on old family patterns. Noticing and releasing patterns that no longer serve you will be an ongoing part of working with your guides.

It's best to get professional support if you're dealing with issues related to abuse or long-term trauma, but asking your guides for support and following simple release practices can help as well. Here's a sequence that works for me.

- Ask for help releasing your fears, known and unknown, that are affecting your life right now. If you know of a specific fear, state it, but don't limit it to what you're consciously aware of. In the lines following each bullet make notes of how you can ask for help.

....

....

....

....

....

....

....

....

....

- Ask to be shielded and protected by Archangel Michael to keep you safe. You can ask for this generally or specifically (while you are driving or traveling, for instance). This helps keep your energy field clear and prevents you from picking up negative energies floating around other people.

....

....

....

....

....

....

....

....

....

- Ask for help to understand the issue and ways you can move beyond it.

....

....

....

....

....

....

....

....

....

....

....

- Ask for help to feel stronger, to know you're capable of releasing and moving past these fears, to feel confident, and to feel the comfort of your guides.

....

....

....

....

....

....

....

....

....

....

....

- Ask for help to know that you're okay just as you are, that you're worthy of guidance, love, help, support, and all good things coming to you.

....

....

....

....

....

....

....

- Ask to be filled with the highest light and love to replace fear, anger, or pain.

....

....

....

....

....

....

....

....

....

....

....

- Give thanks for the help.

....

....

....

....

....

....

....

....

....

....

....

....

Here's an easy ritual that many people do with the full moon. Write down what you want to release on a piece of paper or use one small piece of paper for each thing. Burn the paper(s) while imagining the fear floating off you or dropping away like chunks of dirt in the shower. Drink a glass of cool water, intending that the liquid replace your fear with light.

If you find that reading this brings up fears about being able to release your old patterns or get help, add that to the mix. You don't need to relive the fear or go back into the details of what happened to instill the fear, and you don't need to understand how the guides are helping you release it; just let them help you and let it go.

If you have anger instead of fear, you can use the same approach to letting it go. I've had a lot of anger to release over the years.

What do you think of the comments about a full moon ritual or releasing anger or fear? What do you plan to include at some point in your practice, or what can you do right now?

....
....
....
....

You might have to do this kind of releasing multiple times for a deep fear or stubborn old belief. Each time you release the old patterns that restrict you, you fill up with brighter light in line with the energy of your guides. This process is one of the most important parts of gaining confidence and self-acceptance.

Over time, you'll welcome it when fears come up because you know you can release them, and it feels both comforting and empowering to get it done. That's how I feel when I notice another comment from my internal critics: time to let it go and move on with help at hand.

TRY THIS

What's one old belief or pattern you'd love to be rid of? If you're not sure where to start, think of the most common thing your inner critics say to you and go with that.

....
....
....
....
....

Start tackling it using the notes above to help you. If it's a sticky old one like low self-esteem, it'll pop up differently and you might have to go at it in multiple ways; but keep at it using the Whac-A-Mole approach. You'll look back in six months and be amazed at how much calmer you feel.

....

....

....

....

....

....

....

....

....

....

....

....

....

This work will come in handy in the next chapter as we look at how to get help when life seems to be falling apart around you.

CHAPTER 8: HOW TO GET HELP IN TIMES OF TRAUMA OR TROUBLE

IT CAN BE MOST DIFFICULT to understand that you have help and guides around you when things are going terribly wrong, and you need help right now. The guides are still there, and simple steps can help you get relief right away so you can keep going. It's particularly difficult to sense guidance when you're tense, but that's when you need it most. It helps to have some emergency actions lined up in advance to help you calm down enough to sense guidance or options; you don't want to try to figure it out when you're panicking.

TIPS TO HELP RIGHT NOW

THESE ARE TIPS FOR WHAT to do in an emergency when you can't breathe but need to keep going. Someone you love is sick, you're in financial distress, you're in a place where you don't feel safe, you don't know how to go on: that's when these suggestions will help.

The intention is to get you through the next few minutes so you can calm down enough to ask for help and for you to feel just a bit better right now. Then you can sense the support you're getting and see options or opportunities that you couldn't when you were so tense.

Again, my number one quick fix that you can do anywhere is to take three deep breaths. Not just any breaths, big belly breaths. Tilt back your head, fill up your gut, hold it for a second, breathe out through your mouth, and wait for a second before you inhale again. Do this three times. For me, it's the short pauses after breathing in and out that do the trick and help me get into a rhythm. If you don't feel any relief from this, take three more deep breaths (I do three sets of three and I always feel better). Is this easy? Yes. Free? Yes. Can you easily fit it into your day? Yes. You can even do it right now, as you read or listen. It's the perfect tip!

Research shows the many benefits of deep breathing. I don't want this to turn into a scientific journal article; you can search online and find thousands of links. But for now, I want you to know it strengthens your lungs, lowers your blood pressure, calms your mind, and gets more oxygen to your brain. I keep mentioning this exercise because it works immediately no matter where you are. Check out the book *Breath* by James Nestor and the author's website for more breathing approaches that might be perfect for you.

Here's a list of other emergency relief measures that my students and I have used to feel a little better right away. If there's a repeat from earlier in the workbook, it's because it works here too.

- Call in your guides of highest light and those who can provide emergency support. Say, "I call upon all my guides of highest light. I call upon the support of the archangels and all my guides to help me with (whatever you need: safety for your family, miraculous healing, protection, etc.) right now."

   Revise this to best fit you.

- If you don't even know what to ask for, just say (out loud, if possible), "Help me, I don't know what to do," over and over for a few minutes if you need to. I've done this plenty of times while crying on my knees in my closet when I had no idea what to do, but didn't want the kids to hear me.

    Revise this to best fit you.

....

....

....

....

....

....

....

....

- Do a quick tension release: cry, stretch, rock, and calm your body as you can. You can do this in the bathroom at work or in a hospital if you need to be discreet.
- Tell the guides that you're tense and need their help to be easily understood, immediate, and ongoing. Tell them you need them to be right next to you as you're too stressed to sense them. This is what I do if my kids are in trouble.
- If you're inspired to do something supportive to help whoever is having an emergency, do it. If you're not sensing guidance, do something mildly physical (I clean or fold laundry; a stretch helps too) to release some tension and give yourself a chance to sense any support or guidance that's coming.

95

- If nothing comes, keep calling in help and carry on. There's no problem with continuing to repeat a request until you get some relief.
- I ask myself what I can do to feel a little better right now and do it. Sometimes it's just putting on comfy socks and zoning out. Even feeling a tiny bit better helps. It's better than freaking out or feeling so angry I might blow a blood vessel.
- Get and give some hugs. Do you have a stuffed animal? A young child or pet? Squishy hugs are one of the key things that gets me through tough times.
- Stay hydrated. It's amazing how mild dehydration tires you out and affects your mood. It's easy to forget to drink and eat when you're stressed out or going through a family emergency. The last thing you need is a urinary tract infection on top of everything else.
- Give yourself a small break in whatever way you can: let the house be messy, get takeout, take an extra-long shower, have an ugly cry.
- Go into your car, a closet, or anywhere you have some privacy and let out a good scream, then carry on. Howling at the moon is great, too.
- Let help in and be open to miracles showing up (money, comfort, time, energy, healing, inspiration, etc.). Be open to help coming from other people in unexpected ways.
- Laugh. I have a collection of short videos that I go back to a lot whenever I need a quick laugh. This always helps me feel better.
- Did you create a playlist earlier? You can use that now, too. It's good to build one with a range of songs or create different playlists for different moods. When I'm tense, I need different tunes than I do when I'm tired.

There's a lot here. Note what you think you'd like to try.

....

....

The point of all this is to help you feel just a bit better. It's hard to have a clear head when you feel panic or despair, so do whatever you can to rise above that, even for a few minutes at a time. If you can feel a bit calmer, you'll be able to see a different perspective, remember what you did last time this happened that worked, think of someone who can help, or realize that this is part of an old pattern you don't need to keep repeating. Incremental improvements are the aim of this work.

You can call upon a whole range of helpers when you're in trouble. It's okay to use forceful words when you need to. Try this: "I call upon the assistance of all my guides and all the angelic hosts, ancestor spirits, ascended masters, and star beings of highest light to help me with (whatever) right now. I ask that the assistance continue unceasingly until the issue is resolved. I ask for support, comfort, and clear guidance for me and my family, in line with the free will of all, throughout the duration of this event. I need help right now, please. Thank you."

Revise as best fits you.

HOW TO ASK FOR HELP FOR OTHERS

WHEN SOMEONE YOU LOVE IS ill or in a dangerous situation, it's difficult to think clearly, let alone reach out for help or think about what to say when you ask.

Here's the thing: you can't tell the guides what to do for someone else—regardless of whether it's good or bad—without remembering that we all have free will and are sovereign souls having a human experience. That doesn't mean you can't ask for help on their behalf or send them love from the guides. There are several ways to do this, and I've included scripts to help you start.

Calling in the guides.

Call in all your guides of highest light, and the guides of the other person, in alignment with their free will, and ask for assistance to address the situation. Here's an example.

"I call upon all my guides of highest light, and all of (person's name)'s guides of highest light, in line with their free will. I ask for a miraculous healing of their physical issues, with ease and freedom from pain for their physical, mental, and emotional systems. I ask for their medical team to be guided as well, toward a healing resolution that brings blessings and grace for everyone involved, in alignment with the free will of all."

Revise to best fit you.

....

....

....

....

....

....

Sending light to someone.

You can send light to another person; you just send it to their higher self instead of their physical self. Why? We all have soul lessons that we came in to complete. If someone is experiencing trauma, they might be in the middle of resolving a long-standing issue. We need to give them compassion and the freedom to do this. I know how hard this can be! I've been there several times with family or friends who are critically ill. Here's how you might say this:

"I call upon my guides of highest light and the guides of (name of the other person). I send love to their higher self for the resolution of this situation. I ask that they be wrapped in the highest light and love, surrounded, supported, guided, and protected unceasingly until this situation is resolved in line with their highest good. I ask for support for their family and friends, and I ask that I too be supported as part of this to accept the outcome with compassion and grace. I call upon their guides and mine to give them support, comfort, and freedom from pain and fear throughout this process. I ask the archangels and all their guides to be with them, holding them, and I call in the highest healing and love and blessings. So be it."

Revise to best fit you.

Asking for support for a child.

If you're the parent of a young child or one who is not of legal age, you can request this assistance for them as their parent. You just add that into your initial request: "As the parent of this child, I call forth (whatever guides you're calling)." Then continue with the request as usual. You can also ask for healing of your entire family as part of this process so everyone gets some support, comfort, and love. If you want to ask for assistance for a child who isn't yours, or for an adult child, you can use the same phrasing as noted above for another person, adding in the detail about free will. "I call upon all my guides of highest light, and all of (person's name)'s guides of highest light, in line with their free will. I ask for a miraculous healing of their physical issues, with ease and freedom from pain for their physical, mental, and emotional systems. I ask for their medical team to be guided as well, toward a healing resolution that brings blessings and grace for everyone involved, in alignment with the free will of all."

Revise to best fit you.

| **Supporting someone going through a tough challenge**.

This can be someone who's dealing with a difficult situation such as mental illness, addiction, or ongoing pain and whose condition is making it hard for you to deal with them, but you don't want to cut them out of your life. Please note the other scripts for healing and support that could bring them some help; here's a script to bring some relief and help to both of you.

"I call upon all my guides of highest love and the guides of (person's name). I ask for healing light to surround and support them as they are during (whatever it is, or you can just say 'these difficult times'). I ask for patience and compassion as they deal with this, and I ask that they be guided to address the issues as best they can at this time. May they be blessed with love and support. Please let me know how to continue to hold them and their soul in light, even when it's hard for me to feel this on the physical plane. I ask for solid energetic boundaries around me as I learn how to keep them in my life and maintain my sovereign energetic space at the same time. I also ask for guidance to understand their role and the lessons they bring me in this life, and for support and assistance to release any energies or beliefs I have that contribute, however unknowingly, to their issues or the difficulties between us. I ask for wisdom and grace that we may both experience as much relief and release as possible at this time. Thank you."

Revise to best fit you.

....

....

....

....

....

| **Addressing relationships with love.**

There's an energy practice of sending light to someone's soul when you're having difficulties with them on the physical plane. I use this one a lot, and it's helped multiple times to transform the relationships I have with people. Here's an example: I had a rough childhood, in part due to my mother's parenting style. This probably applies to most of us with one at least one parent, or whoever was or wasn't functioning in a parental role. I wanted to create a more comfortable, less stressful relationship with my mother, but I knew that trying to talk with her directly wouldn't work. So I started sending love to her higher self— nothing on the physical plane, just to her higher self. After a few months of doing this, our relationship changed. She is now more loving and respects my boundaries (usually), and I do the same for her. I've continued to work on this with her for years, whenever I feel it's necessary or helpful, while working on my own issues related to family at the same time. It's always good to look at how I may be contributing, however unknowingly, to a situation.

Is there someone in your life you'd like to try this with? Note who and how you might use the process above.

This is not a one-and-done approach. Think of it as more of a course correction than an immediate solution, and that might help you set your expectations.

When I want to support someone over a long period of time, by keeping them safe, for instance, I will send them love whenever it occurs to me over a period of months. I do this with my sons all the time: I send love to their souls and set the intention for them always to be safe in their homes, while driving, and at work. I set the intention for them to be healthy, happy, and doing what they love while making great money at it. I call in my guides and their guides, and then give thanks.

Is there someone in your life you'd like to try this with? Note who and how you might use the process above.

....

....

....

....

....

....

....

....

....

....

....

....

WHAT TO DO IF NOTHING SEEMS TO BE HAPPENING

I'VE BEEN ASKED WHAT TO do if nothing seems to be shifting and you aren't seeing any results. Here are some things to check.

- Are you open to being guided? Are you asking with a clear and quiet mind and paying attention so you can pick up on possible answers?
- Are you asking for help in a way that details what you need without telling your guides how it should happen? You need to know what you want help with, but it's not your job to tell them exactly how you want it resolved. Remember that resolution, answers, or relief can come without you knowing how or exactly what happened.
- Are you open to receiving help or an answer in unexpected ways?
- Are you asking for another person in alignment with their free will? It could be that their soul has chosen for them to experience this lesson. You can ask for them to be supported, but you can't decide what needs to happen for them.
- Sometimes we have to understand and address a lesson before a situation can be resolved. Do you understand the lesson that's part of what you want help with?
- Sometimes we need to surrender to the timing of a resolution. Let the request go and wait for guidance or an indication of your next step. Believe me, I know how hard this is. I end up asking for help to accept and surrender to the divine timing of the resolution.
- If nothing else works, ask again for guidance to be clear and easily understood, and ask for a sign your guides are with you. Then be open to what happens.

Make note of which of these suggestions might apply to you, and how you plan to use them.

....

....

....

....

....

....

....

....

....

FORGIVENESS

LEARNING TO FORGIVE PEOPLE FOR ways they've harmed me, and letting it go, has been one of the biggest blessings of my life. It's not about accepting what they did, whitewashing it, or pretending it didn't impact me. It's about choosing how to relate to whatever happened so it no longer defines or constrains me.

I'm not glossing over this process; it can take a while, and it can be painful. I am saying that it can be supported and made easier with help from your guides. Their support isn't meant to replace the significant role that therapy can play in this journey, but you can ask your guides to assist you in finding the perfect professional to help.

In my experience, forgiveness creates a huge release of energy and it frees up space in your heart and mind to focus on what's most important to you, so I recommend considering the practice below.

TRY THIS

If this practice sounds like something you'd benefit from, know that it can be used for specific incidents or for a whole relationship. We all have energetic connections with other people, some of them subconscious, and it's good to break and release those that are no longer for our highest good. That's why I'm including text that calls for the breaking of any energetic patterns between you in this sample script.

"I call upon all my guides of highest light, my healing guides, and my guides of compassion and forgiveness for support. I call upon the soul of (name of person). I set the intention that any energetic connections, known or unknown, with (this person) which are not for my highest good be completed now, never to return to me in this lifetime. I set the intention for all my energetic bodies to be healed and sealed from the impacts of these interactions, with ease and grace for all aspects of my being. I set the intention to release any fears, anger, despair, or depression related to their actions, and ask for the healing love of forgiveness to bless me and free me from my outdated connections to them. I ask for the comfort, safety, and security of my guides to surround and support me."

How might you apply this and with whom? This is a big one so take some time with it.

....

....

....

....

....

Forgiving yourself.

This one might be hard for you. It's been a tough one for me. But it gets easier as you as you work with your guides to develop more compassion for yourself and your mistakes. Their nonjudgmental love helps a lot. Here's a script.

"I call upon my guides of compassion and forgiveness. Please help me stop shaming and blaming myself for the mistakes I made. Help me be kind to myself; help me honor the lessons I've learned from my mistakes and the changes I've made as a result. Help me remember that we all make mistakes, I just don't see others' errors in the same critical light I shine on myself. Surround me with comfort and love so I know everything is all right. Help me release these judgments and be at peace with all my past, including my mistakes. Many thanks for your love and guidance."

How might you use this? How does it feel to say this? Take notes.

Asking for forgiveness.

This is a practice used to address energies between you and another person you want forgiveness from. Note: This isn't only for trauma or emergencies; it can be used to heal all of your relationships. It comes from a traditional Hawaiian practice of using forgiveness to bring things back into balance called *ho'oponopono*. This translates as "I'm sorry, please forgive me, I love you, thank you." I use the concepts but not the Hawaiian word since I don't speak the language and I'm not from that culture. Our words have power when we understand them, so it's best to say them in the languages we speak. This approach respects Hawaiian culture as well.

Basically, you connect to someone's energy and ask for forgiveness and resolution of any energies between you related to a certain situation. Here's an example.

"I call upon the higher self of (name of person). For any way that I am connected to you related to (whatever the issue is), I'm sorry, please forgive me, I love you, thank you." You repeat this, with meaning, until you feel some completion. You can do it once or repeat the process multiple times, whatever feels right.

Try this and note how it feels.

I was a single mom and made decisions that I felt were the best at the time but in retrospect were not. My inner critics gleefully jump on these mistakes in the middle of the night or when I'm feeling down about something else. I use this process to address the situation by sending love and light to my kids instead of feeling terrible about myself, and I use it every day.

Here's a script I've used as a parent. Revise it to fit your needs.

"I call upon all my guides of highest light and the higher self of (person). For all the times when I was unavailable because I was working too much or exhausted, for all the times when I was unable to hold you or play with you or give you the attention you needed, I'm sorry, please forgive me, I love you, thank you. For all the times when I didn't realize you weren't getting the support you needed or was depressed and unable to give you the love that I felt, I'm sorry, please forgive me, I love you, thank you."

Revise this script to fit into your life as feels best and as applicable.

TRY THIS

I'm sure you can think of someone you could say this script to. It's an amazing form of healing, release, and empowerment. If nothing else, it frees up your energy so you can direct it positively instead of dwelling on things you wish were different. You can use this generic script for just about anything:

"I call in all my guides of highest light, and I reach out to the higher self of (person's name). For any ways that I am contributing to (issue), I'm sorry, please forgive me, I love you, thank you." Repeat as many times as needed, as often as needed.

Try this, note any changes. How does it feel?

....

....

....

....

....

....

....

....

....

....

....

....

....

I'm spending so much time on forgiveness because it's a powerful release. I do this forgiveness script whenever something I regret or that I'd like to be able to change comes up. Instead of feeling shame about it, judging who I was in the situation, or letting my inner critics dig into me, I send energy to resolve it. That action feels like it transcends time.

The next chapter builds upon our work to help those who are ill or suffering and addresses things we will all experience: death and dying. There's a great deal of help at hand to support us and our loved ones during those transition times.

CHAPTER 9: SUSTAINED SUPPORT DURING ILLNESS, DYING, AND DEATH

Worries and concerns about pain, long-term illnesses, and dying, and fears about what happens afterward, affect all of us in one way or another. I started this chapter with a story that in some ways has a positive ending, but the pain of that loss touches me every day even though I know my brother is at peace.

Whether you came to this chapter directly from the table of contents or are working steadily through the workbook, the practices outlined so far related to learning to ask for and recognize guidance can provide a scaffolding of support during times when it's difficult to think clearly. The practices shared in this chapter are like what I included in the last chapter on trauma and troubles, but more focused on support needed for a long-term issue.

The scripts I share here can also be helpful with many kinds of illnesses, not just physical ones. Severe depression, chronic illness like long COVID-19, dealing with family patterns of poverty consciousness, the psychological impacts of war, sexual violence, and racist or homophobic attacks: all of these too can have sustained impacts on your mental, emotional, and physical bodies, and the practices shared here focus on getting you support as you deal with them in the long-term.

These practices can also be used for issues related to finances, career concerns, or relationship woes—anything you've been dealing with for a while. When I was going through my divorce it felt like part of me was dying, even though divorce was my idea. Outdated beliefs and assumptions about how my life would go, who I was as a woman, what it meant to be loved, and whether I could be loved were all dying, and I leaned into what I share here to support me in that death, too.

This chapter will be heavy on scripts and light on discussion. The fears surrounding these topics can feel so heavy. While they are universal, the ways they appear in our lives are so specific to each of us that I don't want to comment, I just want to share ways to feel support.

The ability of the guides to cocoon us, hold us, bathe us in comfort and love comes to the forefront in their sustaining support, and can be requested to continue unceasingly when that is really needed. Use the basic steps outlined in Chapter 6 to get grounded, create a safe space, and set your intention to get the support you request in ways that are clear and easily understood. Then dive into the scripts.

ASKING FOR HELP WITH ONGOING ISSUES

I ALWAYS START REQUESTS FOR help with the archangels, since it is part of their primary purpose, and they're always around all of us. I call in Archangels Michael, Raphael, and Gabriel for healing and calming. I ask for Kuan Yin and the Goddess Isis to be present if I need serenity and the comfort of knowing I'll have strength to lean into while a situation gets resolved. This helps me, too, when something is out of my hands. Sometimes we must go through a tough time to break a pattern or as part of a lesson, and we may need to allow loved ones to do the same.

When we ask for powerful help, it comes in powerful ways: the arrival of unexpected relief and comfort, miracles popping up, the guides making their presence clearly known. Be open to getting answers to your prayers through the actions of others on the physical plane. Perhaps someone you love is ill and a great doctor or new treatment comes, or they have an unexpected, rapid recovery. Or you get support from a friend or counselor to let a loved one go if they are suffering. Maybe protection arrives when you are feeling unsafe, or money shows up out of the blue to get you through a crisis.

Let's go into some specific scripts for instances like this.

LONG-TERM ILLNESS

Exhaustion, fear, and pain can make dealing with a long-term illness even more difficult. In these instances, you can ask that any support provided by your guides be unceasing and strong enough for relief.

Be open to guidance coming in unexpected ways or through other people, such as new doctors, treatments, or medications. It's important to ask for peace, ease, and freedom from pain, discomfort, and fear. Pay attention to your body, as wisdom and guidance can come through your body or be most easily perceived through your body.

Sometimes you need to be asleep for miracle healings to occur. You can ask for a full range of healing modalities to be applied to your illness, including any healing technologies from star beings. In my experience, it's best to ask for these healings to take place while you are sleeping so your mental processes don't get in the way of their work.

Here's a sample script to begin with. Use what's helpful and ignore what isn't.

"I call upon all my guides of highest light and healing power. I ask for support to find treatments that bring me healing and relief from discomfort, pain, and fear. I set the intention to receive healing using the most advanced techniques available from the full range of healing guides available. I am open and ready to receive miraculous healing. I am open and ready to feel peace and ease as part of my support from all my guides. I ask to understand the lessons behind my illness, and for assistance in addressing any energy patterns related to those lessons so the issues can be resolved, released, and healed. Please help me feel your comfort and love, and the energy and strength to handle the symptoms and issues related to my illness. I am deeply grateful for this support. Thank you."

Revise to fit you, note what works and how it feels.

Ask to be held. Keep asking. Pay attention to any inner critics telling you that healing isn't possible, that you don't deserve to feel better, or that you need to just shut up and bear it. These are limiting beliefs that you can release, and you can ask for help with that.

"I ask to be unceasingly cocooned in light, held in love, guided, and comforted as I heal. I ask for help in understanding how to deal with and heal from this illness and best support my body in the healing process. I ask for help releasing any outdated beliefs and thought patterns related to my ability to heal and be free of pain, discomfort, and fear, and to replace those beliefs with the knowledge that I can receive miraculous healing and that my body is capable of great transformation. I am open to receiving healing on all levels, planes, and dimensions of my consciousness with ease, grace, flow, and joy in my mental, emotional, and physical bodies. Thank you."

Revise to fit you and note how it feels.

TERMINAL ILLNESS

IF YOU OR A LOVED one have received a diagnosis of a terminal condition, you can still use the scripts above and ask for a miracle healing. You can also shift your focus to being free of pain and fear, held, comforted, and guided through the upcoming transition.

It's okay to repeatedly request assistance when you need it. We are the ones in bodies, dealing with all this 3D stuff that the guides don't experience, so when it's important, I call upon the assistance of all the hosts of heaven to attend to someone I love and keep them free from discomfort, pain, and fear. Here's a script to use and revise as best fits your situation.

"I call upon all the hosts of heaven, all healing guides, all modalities, and all treatments to ease, grace, and bless (person's name, or 'me' if this is for you). I request this assistance for freedom from pain and fear, and that your support, comfort, guidance, and love bathe and cocoon them unceasingly, while awake and asleep. May they receive comfort on the physical plane from their medical team. May they be blessed with the remembrance of the beauty and love they have received and given and know that they are deeply loved and held by angels during this time. I ask for the love surrounding them to be so strong that they feel its power to free them of discomfort and fear moving forward. Bless them with ease and comfort. Thank you."

Revise to work for you, how does it feel to use this?

....

....

....

....

....

DYING AND DEATH

I HAVE A STORY TO share that might bring comfort if you or someone dear to you is dying or has passed. I had a private client ask me to have a session with her mother, who was afraid of dying. The client asked me to bring in her mother's guides, talk to them, and share any messages they had. I said yes but wasn't sure she would be open to what came through as she was a devoted Catholic and attended mass every day. Her daughter assured me it would be okay.

When I went into my meditation to call in her guides, I was amazed. I saw a long stream of angels, hundreds of angels, lined up and passing in front of her, placing a hand on her heart and blessing her for her devotion and faith. This went on and on and on. I shared how deeply loved she was, how honored she was for her faith and her commitment, and how blessed she was by the love in her heart. I don't remember all the details, but the vision was astoundingly beautiful. I heard later that she loved it and listened to the recording many times. Her whole family listened and was moved by it. She felt comforted by the session and passed in peace.

We can all pass in peace. Here's a sample script for the process of dying.

"I call forth my guides of the highest light as we move into the transition process, so (person's name) is carried home to the light encased and enrobed in divine grace. I ask this for all levels and planes of their consciousness, mind, body, and soul, in support of their soul's passage back to the light. May they know unceasing peace and ease through this process. May they receive support on the physical plane from their medical team, caregivers, and family to bring them comfort and freedom from pain. I call upon Archangels Michael, Gabriel, and Raphael and their angelic hosts to free them from fear, lift them up, and carry them home, back to the highest light in line with their divine soul mission. May they be blessed by this; may they know their soul's worth and how deeply loved they are. May they transition in full knowledge of their divine beauty and light. Thank you."

Revise this to work for you, write down any thoughts or feelings you have on this.

Love we send someone is never wasted, so you can continue to pray for someone's soul to be supported in moving into their highest expression of light even after they have died.

You can't change what happened to a loved one who passed traumatically, but you can send light to their soul and ask the guides—the Archangels Michael, Gabriel and Raphael and their angelic hosts in particular—to comfort their soul and heal them of residual fears.

GRIEF

YOUR GUIDES CAN SUPPORT YOU in your grieving process, through all of its stages. A popular model of grief considers five stages: denial, anger, bargaining, depression, and acceptance. Another model notes seven stages: shock and denial, pain and guilt, anger and bargaining, depression, the upward turn, reconstruction and working through, and acceptance and hope. No matter which model you think best applies to your situation, asking for support can help you through the entire process.

Grief is held in your body, so incorporating movement and soothing rituals can help you process it and put you in a better position to perceive the help you have right at hand. Here's a general script to help you process and release your grief:

"I'm asking for the help of my guides of highest love. I am in so much pain in my grief. I feel so much anger, guilt, and regret. Please help me understand how to process and release these feelings and how to find the energy to keep going and take care of the things I need to attend to. Please help me sleep, and please help me quiet my mind so I can stop focusing on this. Fill my heart with ease. I ask for guidance that is easily perceived and understood, and to be unceasingly held in love as I begin to heal. Please bring me inspiration and support on the physical plane as part of this process, too. Thank you. I am grateful for the help."

Take note of your thoughts and feelings on this, and ways you can use this in your life to help you or someone in your life process grief.

SETTING AN INTENTION FOR YOUR OWN DEATH

ARE YOU AFRAID OF DYING? Many people are. But it can be a time of great blessing and freedom from pain, constraints, worries, and fears. You can set an intention to be supported and carried home to the light and repeat this whenever you feel worried or afraid. Here's a script.

"I call upon all my guides to help me release my fears of dying. I set the intention to be free of fear and pain as I transition out of this body. I ask that any old patterns of judgment and fear of rejection I have related to dying be released now and replaced with the clear knowledge and trust that I am deeply loved, worthy of love, and moving back to the love that I came from. I ask that I be carried home to the light in beauty, joy, and remembrance of the glory of my soul. May I be blessed in my transition as I return to those I love who have gone before me. Please hold me close, carry me, comfort me, and bring me to grace. Thank you."

Note your thoughts and feelings about your own death and using this or a similar scripts to help you.

SETTING THE INTENTION FOR A POSITIVE AGING PROCESS

ARE YOU PLANNING FOR A joyful last phase of your life? What does your body want to share with you about the process? If you fear you might be stiff and have limited mobility, work on increasing your flexibility and incorporate stretches and other practices now that will support your body more. Are you worried about your mental processes? What a gift the internet is for us, so we can research the latest developments and tried-and-tested tips related to cognitive resilience.

Take notes on this, spend a few minutes thinking about all this and ways you can set intentions and take actions.

....

....

....

....

....

....

What else are you worried about? Finances? Ask the guides to bring you financial experts to support you, and tell them to bring more abundance your way, too. Check your assumptions and old family patterns here: Are you assuming, because of what your family says and believes, that your life must end in poverty and fear? You know better than that now; you can ask for help and be proactive about releasing those beliefs and setting an intention to have a healthy, happy, joyful, creative, free, inspiring, sovereign, expansive life in the time remaining to you.

Choosing to be positive and proactive about what we want and creating a life that supports this is a rebellious act, and it's a revolutionary act in the face of all the fear and negative messages about aging. It anchors energy for living life differently and helps others access the power to create the lives they want.

I intend to fulfill my potential for joyful creativity and share as much love as I can with people and the planet for the rest of my life. I intend to embody the energies and power of the Divine Feminine to my fullest capacity, to create a more just and peaceful world. That's how I'm planning the remaining time I have on Earth. How about you?

Spend a few minutes thinking of this last page and your thoughts on your life and your plans for the remainder of your life. Write, draw, scribble, paint.

This was a heavy chapter. Let's have a palate cleanser in the next one, which is all about how to find more ease, flow, and joy in your life through working with your guides.

CHAPTER 10: MORE EASE, FLOW, AND JOY

I SHARE DETAILS AND SCRIPTS below so you can begin to incorporate more ease, flow, and joy into your life. When you hang out with your guides, your vibration naturally rises to be in closer resonance with theirs; you harmonize with them (you're in resonant harmony with them). Not completely, but there's a definite increase in the light and love you carry inside you.

This makes everything easier. Lower, negative energies and patterns can't cling to you, and you recognize them more quickly. You're better equipped energetically to call in support and to recognize it—it's like tuning a radio from static to a station with a strong reception.

You can ask for help to raise your frequency as you ask for the other support you need. And when you're feeling good, ask for help to sustain it. The main difference between what I share in this chapter and what we've looked at earlier in the workbook is that these practices help sustain what feels great, what we appreciate, and what keeps us going.

I've pulled together topics and approaches below that we haven't covered yet so you can see additional ways to apply what we've already covered, and work with the guides who are already around you to help make your life a little better every day.

Let's dig in so you can see what I mean and start using what seems fun.

DAILY PRACTICES FOR STAYING BALANCED AND SERENE

IN THIS SECTION, I SHARE specific things I do every day to stay balanced and serene (for the most part). It's not necessary to do all of them—see what works best for you.

Mantras.

A mantra is a word or phrase used to put your mind in a calm, meditative state. A simple mantra can help you maintain your positive outlook and address your desires with confidence. I use mantras to focus my thoughts and energy on what's important to me, and to set up the vibration of what I want but might not have yet.

Two short mantras I use throughout the day are "Everything's all right" and "I'm fully supported in all ways and always."

I created a long, rhythmic mantra to use while I'm walking the dog. You could use parts of this or take it as inspiration to create your own walking mantra. Here it is.

"I'm so richly blessed and abundantly free,
I always have so much more than I need.

In opulent flow, I create joyfully.
I always have all the inspiration I need.

With my family and guides so supportive of me,
I always have all the love I need.

I'm vibrantly healthy, limber, and lean.
I always have all the youthful energy I need.

In restful repose, I relax gracefully.
I always have all the time I need.

I'm so blessedly rich, sovereign, and serene.
I always have all of everything I need."

TRY THIS

What mantra might work for you? It could be one word or phrase, or you could use an image associated with a word to bring yourself peace. You could create a longer mantra like I did (or use whatever parts of mine you like). You can find traditional mantras connected with yogic or religious practices online, or you look for other affirmations or phrases that calm you.

....

....

....

....

....

....

....

....

....

....

Manifesting.

Many people focus on manifesting what they want by deliberately choosing thoughts, feelings, and energy that are in alignment with what they want—the energy of already having it. You may have heard this referred to as "deliberate creation" or "following the law of attraction." It ties into what we talked about earlier in the workbook: holding a vision of what you want, feeling and imagining that it's already true, and adding sensory details to the vision so you resonate more closely with what you want. You aren't searching for it, grasping at it, or hoping it will come true; you are embodying how it feels when you have it, luxuriating in it.

You can imagine what you want to manifest (a new job, money for a home, a healthy family, someone who loves you just as you are) and call in the support of your guides at the same time to not only help make this dream come true, but also help you raise your vibration so you can align more quickly with the desired end result. This works for everything:

- Flow
- Creativity
- Financial abundance
- New opportunities
- Loving relationships
- A happy family
- Vibrant health
- Travel and adventure

TRY THIS

Here's a script for manifesting.

"I call upon all my guides of highest light to support me in creating and maintaining a vibration of having (what you want). Help me hold the energy, images, feeling, and sense of already succeeding in having this. Help me hold the perfect degree of focus, keeping the energy flowing toward the creation of what I want and sustaining it without striving or worrying about it. Please help me understand and act in ways that support the joyful creation and experience of what we're manifesting together. Thank you."

Play with this and revise to make it work for you.

....

....

....

....

....

....

....

....

....

....

....

....

....

....

....

....

Here's another one to try:

"I call upon all the beings of highest light who work with me. I set the intention to be energetically supported as I imagine having/being (whatever you're looking to manifest). Please help me to manifest this as I imagine it or even better, and to do it with ease, grace, flow, and joy. Please bring me inspiration and ideas for how to manifest my wishes quickly and joyfully. I'm grateful for the support and ask that it continue unceasingly until I receive what I'm drawing to me."

FEELING GRATITUDE AND PEACE

THE FOLLOWING PRACTICES AREN'T THINGS I do with my guides or ask them about, they're part of what I bring to the table when I collaborate with my guides and part of what I do to raise my vibration to carry more light so I'm a good partner in the work we do together. Plus, these practices just help me get through each day feeling as positive as possible.

Feeling grateful.

This is a huge one for me. I've lived in places where life is extremely difficult for people, especially women and children, where they don't have clean air or water or access to food, education, or safety.

How easy I have it—clean water and air, access to food, freedom of speech. Everyone I love is safe and healthy. I can explore and create as I please. I have many opportunities to freely share my writing and spiritual thoughts. And so many choices.

I don't have a specific gratitude practice as much as a running thread of giving thanks throughout the day. Notice what makes life easier for you and what brings you joy or safety.

Gratitude is another high-frequency emotion, so the more you feel it, the closer you get to your guides' resonance of love and light and the more they can help you.

Note what you're grateful for and how you can create a gratitude practice.

....

....

....

....

| Creating.

I get grumpy and frustrated if I'm not using my energy in creative ways almost every day. That can be through cooking, writing, dancing, playing music, or gardening.

Anything I do that creates beauty or joy counts for me (so dancing fits, even though I just do it for fun). Even planning for the creation counts, like reading a new cookbook or planning a new writing adventure. For me, creativity is one of the keys to staying centered in my heart and sustaining a positive flow of love in my life. How about you? What works for you?

Being in nature.

A great deal of my serenity comes from being in nature, sitting in my garden, watering plants, and feeding and watching the birds. Even watching nature documentaries and whale-watching videos or reading articles about nature sustains me. I studied forestry because trees are my favorite thing. Does nature calm and sustain you, too? If not, maybe there are other forms of beauty that do.

Appreciating beauty.

Another thing I make time for is mini beauty breaks. These can include wearing one of my vintage perfumes, watching a movie I love, reading the words of a great writer, getting lost in a story, or looking at home decorating or gardening magazines (don't judge). I make time for all of these things because they fuel me. When I downsized my home after the kids moved out, I curated my belongings so there is now something beautiful that I love everywhere I look, in every room. Does beauty fuel you, or is it something else? I include laughter and hugs in the beauty break category as they bring me joy (which to me is an expression of beauty).

Being the Queen Me.

This is my practice of feeling serenely sovereign. A few years ago, I realized that what I really wanted was to feel serene. Serenely wealthy, too, which for me is knowing that I always have all the resources I need to do everything I want (including time, money, creativity, power, health, energy, and focus). At the time, I didn't know what it would feel like for my normal reality to be fully resourced, so I binge-watched *The Crown* on Netflix. If anyone expects that it's normal to have a life of abundance, it's a queen.

So what happened? I tried on this vibe and discovered that I could lean into the support of my guides more easily. I found and moved into the most perfect place to live. I settled into a creative flow with my writing. I now feel richly blessed and blessedly rich. I am being the Queen Me—blissfully, creatively, serenely, and radiantly. Asking, "How can I feel serenely sovereign as I move through my day?" is now a part of my usual practice.

TRY THIS

What fuels and sustains you? What occurred to you as you read my notes above? What fuels your joy? Squeeze some of these into your day or add them to your practice if that helps.

HANGING OUT WITH GUIDES

IT'S NOT ALWAYS ABOUT WORKING on something or releasing old patterns and beliefs; just hanging out with them and resting in their energy renews me and fills me with peace. Continuing to expand and explore how much light and love I can carry in my body and looking at ways I can support people and the planet will be a daily focus with my guides for the rest of my life.

All of the practices outlined in this workbook help me focus my time and energy on what's most important to me while knowing I'm safe, supported, and free to expand and create in whatever ways feel joyful and powerful to me.

It's about choice: choosing to sense the light that's hidden from our visible world, choosing to feel supported even if I don't see a presence standing in front of me, choosing to trust in my intuition when it might not make logical sense, and choosing to believe that the world can be different, more just and equitable, and infused with pure love. I make these choices every day because I just can't accept that our external reality is all that's available and true.

Note your thoughts on how you can choose to spend time with the guides and use your energy.

....

....

....

....

....

....

Here's an affirmation I use at the beginning of the day to orient myself.

"I am an emanation of the divine light. I open now to receive that which by my divine destiny is given from the source of loving creation. I am an emissary of light. I open now to be all that I am, and to allow the manifestation of these divine gifts to fully flow through me for the wellness of the world, the wellness of my own body, and the loving presence of the divine light at work in my life. This is my affirmation of the light, and the invocation of my intention, manifest on all levels, planes, and dimensions of my consciousness. So be it."

Revise this or create an affirmation to use in your practice.

TRY THIS

What process can you use to keep expanding your light and love in the world? How can you collaborate with your guides to take advantage of all the blessings and ease that are already in your life? You can use what I shared above, or here's another script to get you started.

"I call upon my guides of highest love to help me orient my day and energy to what feels truest to me and serves my highest good, no matter what's showing up on the news or in my life. I choose to trust in the love I sense from my guides and the truth of my intuition, and I ask for ongoing support in finding ways to share my soul gifts and strengths freely and joyfully. Thank you."

Make notes and revise the script as best for you.

The next chapter builds upon these concepts and uses your imagination to create an inner sanctuary. It isn't necessary to use an inner sanctuary to work with your guides, but it's something I treasure about my own practice, so I included it.

CHAPTER 11: CREATE YOUR INNER SANCTUARY

An inner sanctuary is a safe space you imagine where you can go for a quiet break or for active work with your guides to receive inspiration, comfort, and answers. It's just using your imagination to envision a place where you can interact with your guides, especially if sitting in quiet meditation doesn't work for you. It never has worked for me, so I meet them in my inner sanctuary.

Creating this space is not necessary for working with your guides or understanding guidance, but my students enjoy learning about it. If it doesn't sound interesting to you, you can skip this chapter. If you enjoy playing with your imagination, you might love it.

If you've found that a walking meditation or some other type of physical activity works best for you to commune with your guides, look at the second option under "Geometric Shape Sanctuary," as this can be a fun way to approach setting an energetic boundary. I use it when I want to make sure I'm not absorbing other people's energy.

THE POINT OF THIS IS PLAYFUL POWER

Basically, the inner sanctuary is a space or feeling you imagine in enough detail that you can return to it again later. The point is to create a space where you feel completely safe and able to turn off the world and turn up your imagination. When you allow your imagination free rein, you begin to feel the playful power of your expanded self, filling you up with luscious possibilities.

You can use your sanctuary to take a break from the stress of outer life and/or to let your mind, heart, and joyful creativity expand free of constraints. You can make it as simple as a quiet beach, a pair of rocking chairs on a porch, or however your imagination wants to run with.

HOW YOUR IMAGINATION AND AN INNER SANCTUARY CAN HELP YOU

IF YOU ENJOY USING YOUR imagination, your willingness to experiment with it can be the cornerstone of your spiritual practice. This can be so effective in your search for inner answers because as you gain peace and receive guidance in the sanctuary, you begin to experience the same things in your external life. As you release limiting patterns, ancestral beliefs, and fears of your creative power in the sanctuary, you start to move through your days of laundry, cooking, and working with the same sense of release and inspiration.

SETTING EXPECTATIONS

THIS MAY TAKE MORE TIME than anything else in the workbook, depending on how detailed you get and how easy it is for you to imagine. It takes more time because you are, in essence, building an energetic container to hold the frequency of your guides and your soul. It's a resonance chamber.

Because it takes repeated exposures to their frequencies to instill the energies of the guides in a space, it's not something you do once and check off a list. The buildup of resonance is the reason this practice can become so helpful, even if you just imagine sitting in the space. It's like a sauna of higher love without the heat.

You might jump right into this. Most of us work at visualizing a sanctuary space for a while to make it feel substantial and real and to anchor the details that support our experience. My students love entering my sanctuary in meditations, but not all of them end up using a sanctuary in the long run. That doesn't stop them from working with their guides.

I share this practice as it's been so effective and fun for me. You might want to read or listen to the whole chapter first and then come back to what seems intriguing and enjoyable for you to explore. Now that I've made you either warier or more curious, let's jump in.

CREATING YOUR INNER SANCTUARY

THIS BEGINS WITH IMAGINING A peaceful place that feels safe and calm. You make the place seem as real as possible. If you've visited a place like this on a vacation or from a favorite book in childhood (*The Secret Garden* is one example), you can just use that. The first step to creating your inner sanctuary is to find this place of peace, a landing area where your mind can rest and rejuvenate, a seat of solace. If spaces don't bring you peace, jump to the next section covering geometric shapes.

Find images that bring you the greatest peace and hold them so strongly in your mind that, with your eyes closed, you can see yourself experiencing this peace. Build in as many details as possible: what it looks like, smells like, and sounds like; the weather and the amount of sunlight; sounds from the wind, birds, or animals; how it feels to be there, what you're wearing, and where you're sitting or walking. Make it real. The more real it feels, the better it can serve you as a space for interacting with your guides.

Remember the vision of the future we started with? I'd like you to call up that vision, that feeling of being calm, confident, clear, able to create what you want, and fully receptive to guidance and the answers you seek, and we'll build upon that.

Make notes of your vision for reference as you begin creating your inner sanctuary – draw, paint, use stickers, images or a mind map – whatever frees your imagination.

Once you've chosen your place of peace, I want you to imagine there's a short path leading away from it to a wall with a gate in it. See yourself walking up the short path to the gate. The wall is high enough that you can't see into the area. You open the heavy door, and the most beautiful, protected space is revealed, with a building that fits into the setting so perfectly it draws you in.

Look around: This is a place where you can feel safe, a space for inspiration, working with your guides, and dreaming of how you'll create a life and world you love. Stay here, rest here, and fill in as many details as seem fun right now. This isn't the only version of your sanctuary—you might find that the building gains rooms or the gardens and landscape expand—but feel a joyful peace here now. It's a great start.

....

....

....

....

....

....

....

....

....

....

Each time you want to return to this sanctuary, you can either start at the place where you began or close your eyes, touch your heart, and imagine you are immediately in the walled-in area. You will be—or you will be eventually, with practice. Don't put pressure on yourself to get that part instantly right. Your sanctuary is meant to be a playful, peaceful place, so sink into that and let it bless you.

If moving out of the initial peaceful place feels like a tug and you want to stay there, you can imagine some type of structure or space there. If you're on a beach, you can simply add a cave you can enter as your place of interaction. You might have structures there as well, like a tent, a cathedral, or a house with a courtyard and fountain. Use whatever imagery you find most inspiring and fun that pops easily into your imagination.

You can also ask your guides to help you imagine a space where it will be easiest for you to work together.

Make notes on what you're creating or sensing.

TRY THIS

Think about these questions and see what comes to mind.

- What images bring you great peace? The trigger for your sanctuary is not just beauty, but peace.
- What is your landscape, soundscape, or capsule of calm and serenity?
- How do you move through it? Are you resting in a shelter and looking out at it or walking in gracious gardens?
- How does water play a part in your sanctuary? How about fire, trees, scents, sounds, or the wind? Are there forests and animals in this space, or just a pristine structure?

YouTube videos, Instagram posts, and Pinterest images can be a source of inspiration here if you're a visual person or don't like to do quiet meditation. If you really enjoy playing with this, you can create many spaces in your sanctuary to support you. In my temple, there are many places to explore:

- A library with volumes of books and a massive table where the guides gather with me for teaching.
- A bathhouse and steam room for healing and releasing old patterns.
- A meadow with large oak trees where I lie in the grass and relax under a beautiful sky.
- A large home where I meet with a group of goddesses.
- Gardens to wander in (nature is obviously important to me).
- A large safari tent that looks out onto a savanna where I write and talk with my creative muses.

I work with a wide range of guides in my sanctuary in support of my dreams and creativity and as part of my work for the planet. I created a resource page on my website that includes a link to images for a sanctuary space or imaginarium. Check it out at https://julesapollo.com/extras if you'd like some inspiration.

IF THIS APPROACH DOESN'T WORK FOR YOU

MAYBE YOU'RE NOT AS VISUAL. Maybe the sense of touch is more important for you, and you imagine a sauna or a pool with water at the perfect temperature for relaxing. Maybe walking meditations work best for you, and you just check in, imagine your guides walking next to you, and allow inspiration to flow in.

I had a student who'd survived great trauma and didn't feel safe outside, even imagining being outside. We finally discovered that seeing herself within a golden sphere of protection from Archangel Michael while sitting on her bed, allowed her imagination to soar.

Something I've done during stressful times is close my bedroom door and call in the guides to surround me on my bed, telling them they have to come close as I'm too stressed out to do anything else. This might be perfect for you—if so, run with it.

If none of this works, there are videos on YouTube with sound and imaginary spaces—such as a cabin in a snowstorm or an old library with a roaring fire, the sounds of birds in a forest, or a rainstorm from inside a tent—that might be a place to start. You could go from there or just use the source video if that works.

Perhaps you're not visual but music or sounds really help you relax and enter expanded states. You can create a soundscape as an opening for guidance. It could include the sound of the ocean, songs of whales or birds, gentle rain, or a breeze through a forest. There are many soundtracks you can get—YouTube can be a great place to try different ones to see what you like—and you can purchase MP3s of hour-long rainstorms, for instance, quite inexpensively. I know many artists and authors who write while listening to specific soundtracks. I like to put on a soundtrack of whale songs when I'm moving through an airport to create a calming soundscape around me.

There's no need to go down a rabbit hole of research on this. It's best to start with whatever first entered your mind as you were reading this section that gets you to a place of peace so you can sense guidance.

Does anything in this section appeal to you? Note how you might use these suggestions in your practice at different times, and note anything you find through online research that you'd like to incorporate into your practice.

....

....

....

....

....

....

....

....

....

....

....

....

If this approach seems silly or doesn't appeal to you, let's review the next one, as it's a completely different way of getting the same result.

GEOMETRIC SHAPE SANCTUARY

THIS IS AN APPROACH TO creating a safe space and sanctuary within an imagined, clear geometric shape or shelter you rest within. I use a sphere or a pyramid. This is an old spiritual practice, and many people use a cube called "the cube of space" to do this with different guides who are called in from each side of the cube. Read on to see what I mean: the guides describe it better than I can.

TRY THIS

First, choose a form to sit inside. I always use a sphere if I'm walking and a pyramid if I'm sitting, for no reason other than that's what I like. Let it settle, play with the size and the clarity of the materials for a bit. You can add light moving through the sides if this makes sense or leave it out. I usually don't see lights but rather intend for the form to be infused with the light and protective love of the archangels. I put a sphere around me if I'm going through a busy public space like a shopping mall or an airport and don't want to pick up energy from others. If you're an empath, someone who is sensitive to the energy of others, this is an easy way to preemptively protect yourself.

Notes on the shape you've chosen and how this feels when you try it out.

You can combine this imagery with the imagery of your sanctuary. I envision myself sitting in a crystal pyramid on a secluded beach with the soft sounds of waves in the background when I need to quickly calm my mind and body. This is one of the more playful ways to find some inner peace and get guidance, so have fun.

These peaceful places have sustained me in both joyful and difficult times and are part of the true power of this work for me. The next chapter talks about how you've changed since starting this workbook, what that means for making your big dreams and goals come true, and how you can help people and the planet in ways you may not have thought about before, the true power of this work for you.

CHAPTER 12: HOW YOU'VE CHANGED AND WHAT YOU CAN DO WITH IT

I'M NOT ONE OF THOSE spiritual people who never gets angry. These times fill me with rage at not being able to make a bigger impact or limit people's suffering, especially children's. Recently I was meditating on peace but got frustrated. It didn't feel like enough. I asked my guides for help, and here's what they said.

Become incandescent with your rage at the suffering of people and the planet. If that doesn't feel powerful enough, imagine your rage as light eruptions, geysers of light, tsunamis of light: the earth's power to reset and clear can be a guide and example at this time. Your light triangulates with the light of those you've called forth to reset energies, patterns, and light grids so they are infused with love and not the fears of small men driving patriarchal patterns. We are present here now. Call in, tap into, expand into the energies and help at hand to construct a new earth.

I love this message; I love hearing how we can use our rage proactively and work with our guides to change the world instead of feeling like we're stuck on the sidelines while it implodes. Here's a script I created from this message that I use when meditating on peace and the changes I feel are needed to create a just and sustainable earth.

"I am that I am. I call in all my guides of the highest light and love. I set the intention to anchor, into the air, the soil, and the waters, the power and love of a thousand suns to transmute the energies of war, genocide, injustice, hatred, and fear into a planetary grid of light so fiercely intense that it eclipses patriarchal patterns of control, illuminating Earth as a healthy and peaceful planet. So be it and so it is done."

Try this out, change it to fit your life and how you'd like to help people and the planet now.

....

....

....

....

....

....

....

....

....

....

....

....

....

....

....

....

I always ask for help from my guides to start shifting my energy when I'm frustrated. I limit my time on social media, so I can track what's going on in the world but leave once I start to get upset and before I dive into despair, which is a debilitating emotion for me. I note what's got me upset, and that's what I work on with the guides. Together, we anchor light to override lower energies and infuse the world with love and peace. This uses the support we all have at hand to help create a new reality.

Now that you have the tools to work with your guides, I hope you'll use these tools to help make the world a better place. You're here now on this planet, in the middle of all this chaos, to call use your energy and guides to help, so dig into this.

Here are the basic steps you can take.

- Note what's frustrating, angering, or hurting you about the state of the world now.
- Call in all your guides of the highest love.
- Set the intention for your combined energies and love to offset and override the conditions and actions you feel need to change to help people and the planet.
- Imagine all types of guides surrounding the planet, coming to help. See hosts of angels or lightships or massive groupings of spacecraft like those in Star Wars, whatever helps you feel there is power behind the energy you're calling in to help, light flowing into the planet to create lasting change.
- Keep coming back to this process whenever you find yourself frustrated, angry, or fearful.
- Trust that your intention and these energies are helping.

Make notes of your thoughts on the bullet list above and how you can use this process or something similar in your life.

Are there actions you can take on the physical plane that pop into your head as you're doing this? Perhaps you can donate to causes, call your representatives, follow organizations that are helping, protest, or create art that expresses what you're feeling and envisioning.

Write down any notes or thoughts on taking action.

....

....

....

....

....

....

....

Don't focus only on the negative actions causing you pain; make sure you use your love and the energy of your guides to imagine a better way. Again, use the phrase "what if." What if we lived on a peaceful planet where everyone's basic needs were met, where everyone had access to education and opportunities to share their gifts, wisdom, and creativity?

....

....

....

....

....

....

....

What if the earth and the environment were respected and honored, and humanity learned from the wisdom and compassion of native cultures to live in harmony with nature?

....

....

....

....

....

....

How can you use 'what if' to imagine a better world?

....

....

....

....

....

....

....

Don't let your mind tell that you this is childish and not worth doing. Nothing has ever been created, invented, or built that wasn't first imagined and held as a viable vision.

My focus now and for the remainder of this life is to expand into embodying more of the exuberance of my soul. To be joyfully creative. To know that the power of the love I have in my heart for my friends and family, the compassion I have for those who suffer from inequality and a lack of adequate resources, and my commitment to the planet are all supported, empowered, anchored, and enlivened as I work with all my guides, my Family of Light, to fulfill my potential and be of service.

How about you?

....

....

....

....

....

....

....

....

....

What you've read so far will help you get guidance in ways that best fit into your life and to trust the guidance you're getting. Once that happens, you'll start to feel some of what I described above because you'll embody more of your soul light, strengths, and power. Here's what I hope you come to know as truth and part of your everyday life:

- You're never alone; help is at hand whenever you need it.
- No matter what happens in your life, you have help to handle it.
- You're deeply loved, supported, guided, and held.
- You're worthy of being loved and of all good things coming to you.

You're not the same person who picked up this workbook, even if you didn't try everything and still wonder what you're sensing.

You have the tools to quiet your inner critics, forgive yourself, and rally support for every aspect of your dreams and goals. But it goes beyond that. You've had an operating system upgrade and it's time to put that to use. You're stronger, more resilient, and more aware of the ways you can apply the help at hand. You're in resonance with the guides around you.

The planet is messed up. Whole countries are in chaos and suffering is everywhere. Being an embodied soul at this time of great upheaval is a gift and a responsibility. There are many souls lined up, hoping for the chance to become embodied on the planet during these times of massive transformation, even for short periods of time.

You won the embodiment lottery. And now you can be an energy resistance worker by calling in peace, justice, and compassion with your morning coffee and seeing these energies fill up the planet like water in a well. Calling in the support of your guides, you can set the intention for your energy and time to be focused on activities and people in line with your integrity and core values so that where you shop, how you communicate, the work you do, and the flow of your days are all true to the light and wisdom of your soul.

Feeling joyful and creative is a subversive act when the powers running the world want you to feel anger and fear. Love, joy, bliss, and compassion are exponentially more powerful than hatred or fear due to the difference in their frequencies. Choosing to spend at least a part of your day flowing with the energy of your soul and resting in the enveloping love of your guides can be a massive contribution to a more peaceful planet, even if it's in small increments over time.

If nothing else, intend to start your day filled with peace and to move through the day as a beacon of peace, a lighthouse, an embodied star. Anchor peace in your home and garden, as you drive your car or take transit, and every time you interact with someone. Hosts of enlightened beings are ready to help you anchor that light to start changing the world.

It's going to take all of us showing up to heal the planet. Be subversively spiritual and let your love erupt exuberantly from your heart. Let it be boisterously incandescent.

How can you be subversively spiritual, exuberantly expansive? How can you use the help of your guides to create a better world in line with your intentions, passions, skills and strengths?

PART 2

EXPERIMENTING

THE POINT OF THIS SECTION is to play with how to best work with your guides. Trying things out, noting what happened, and tweaking. Here's another script to try out when you start experimenting.

"I call upon all my guides of highest light. I'm trying to find the best way to work with you and create a practice that fits into my life. Help me figure out what's easiest, help me understand the guidance I'm getting. Bring me urges and inspiration for things to try that will be of greatest benefit. Help me understand how to experience your energy and support. Thank you."

Change this script to work best for you.

The following pages include space for you to note your thoughts, ideas, and inspirations. Use colored pencils or gel pens, stickers, images cut out from magazines, mind maps or sketches to free up your thinking and consider more options.

This part covers three topics:

- Creating Your Practice
- Release and Renewal Rituals
- More Joy

CREATING YOUR PRACTICE

TAKE THESE QUESTIONS AS PROMPTS for journaling, mind mapping, or planning out ways you will experiment with what works best to help you create a bespoke practice with the perfect fit for your days and life now. Don't worry about answering each question as you read it, this bullet list is followed by a few blank pages for you to experiment with and refine your practice.

- How is the beginning process working for you: breathing, setting space, feeling grounded?
- Try a few different times of day to see what works best for your energy and document it.
- How have you been able to squeeze in time to work with your guides? Note successes or things you're still adjusting.
- Try walking or moving and then talking with guides, or asking a question and then doing something physical. Keep your phone or a notebook with you in case you start getting inspired and want to record notes.
- Ask questions you have before bed and note any dreams you remember when you wake up (it's best to note these before you get out of bed, or you'll forget).

- Play with different deep breathing techniques, see what works best.
- Pick three possible practices from the list provided in Chapter 7 to calm down. Document progress and any changes you made or things you're doing to change.
- Check out the playlists from https://julesapollo.com/extras and see if any of this music helps to support your practice. Do these playlists help, or have you created your own playlist?
- How can you work with your guides as a project manager, assigning tasks and creating deadlines (while you do your own inner work to allow inspiration to be easily perceived and acted upon)?
- Notice any ways your inner critics are limiting your approach to creating a practice. Include ways to quiet their voices as a normal part of your practice (don't think of their presence as an indication this won't work for you).
- When thinking about your dreams and goals, how can you build upon your curiosity, enthusiasm, and passion to energize your work?

187

RELEASE AND RENEWAL RITUALS

RELEASE AND RENEWAL RITUALS CAN be small actions you do each day, with the phases of the moon, or seasonally. They can be as simple as a weekly visioning session of the future when your dreams have come true, spending time creating and visiting your inner sanctuary, or doing a simple tarot reading looking at what needs to be released to help you fulfill your potential. You can include physical activities as part of rituals: dancing, stretching, walking, cooking, painting, or other creative activities.

The reason this section includes both releases and renewals together is because you'll find that as you progress through your spiritual journey that both are needed. You will keep coming up against old patterns that no longer fit, so having an efficient process for release is useful. These old patterns frequently drain your energy so having a few tried and true renewal practices will be handy too. You can try out different approaches for both below.

Getting Started.

Do you like rituals? Do you need some ideas for simple rituals that could support your spiritual practice? Lighting a candle or some incense at the beginning of working with your guides can be a way for your practice to feel sacred and special. Use whatever feels easiest as you're getting your practice started. You can download apps that help you turn off the rest of your digital world and focus for a few minutes. There are many options.

- Note the outcomes of different rituals you use to connect with your guides. Meditating in the bathtub, lighting a candle, using yoga stretches before you start, and always working with your guides in the same location can help get your mind and body relaxed and quiet so you can perceive subtle sensations more easily.

- Ask for special support in line with the energies surrounding phases of the moon, solstices, equinoxes, etc., and explore rituals that celebrate these events with your guides.
- Take a ritual bath or a swim with the intention to release any outdated energies. You can choose a special soap with a scent you love and wear a favorite perfume afterwards, the scents becoming part of the release and renewal process over time.
- Call in your guides to assist you with whatever release and renewal you feel would be helpful or ask them to guide you to what is needed for your highest good and do it with the intention that it all be completed with ease, grace, flow, and joy.

Use these ideas on rituals along with the specific scripts below to help you release whatever's holding you back so more of you can shine.

Tarot Cards and Oracle Decks.

Using tarot cards and oracle decks is a great way to support your practice and to start getting answers to questions right away as you're still trying to understand how to best work with your guides. I use these decks frequently to get clarity and to reinforce what I'm sensing in meditations. It's easy to find decks you enjoy holding and looking at with an emphasis on an aspect of spirituality that's meaningful for you, such as nature-based decks or those with inclusive imagery, for example.

It's important to set your intention for the cards (just stating what you'd like help with and the number of cards). For instance, I'm looking for three cards of guidance for the coming week: who I am, what's going on, what needs to be integrated (or what's coming). It's your choice, you just need to let the cards know. It's like placing an order for takeout: you need to specify what you want. If you don't have a specific need, it's ok to just say a general phrase such as 'guidance for the week'.

I write down my weekly readings in my journal and usually refer to them during the week as things come up for context and as a reminder of what to focus on and what can help to resolve situations or energies that have shown up.

Here are some simple ways to use the cards (either tarot or oracle cards or a combination of decks work for these).

- Pull one card for daily guidance in the morning or before going to bed as a focus for your dreaming or for what to focus on the next day (use whichever time frame works best for having a few peaceful, pensive minutes).
- A weekly 3-card spread: who you are, what's going on, and what's the outcome if you address what's in card 2. You can pull a fourth card if you want more clarity on what needs to be addressed as part of card 2.

- Pull two cards: one for who you are now, and one for what the cards want to tell you. I use this a lot when I'm working with more than one deck to get a broad perspective (and because I like a lot of decks but I'm too impatient to pull multiple cards from more than one deck).
- My weekly practice is a 3-card reading with the Gentle Tarot (my favorite deck) and then a couple of 2-card readings with several other favorite decks. You can find a list of the tarot and oracle decks I use here: https://julesapollo.com/extras (there's more than a dozen and I'm sure I'll get more, I love playing with the cards). I'm no tarot expert, so there are a couple of recommended books about tarot included on the website. Here are some current favorites:
  - The Gentle Tarot
  - The Wild & Sacred Feminine Oracle
  - The Sacred Forest Oracle
  - The Radiant Tarot
  - Woodland Wardens Oracle

Here are a couple of pages to try out these cards and note your thoughts, you might want to keep track of the cards you pull in your regular journal or a separate journal for the cards you pull to track over time.

I created two layouts you can use when you'd like to get input from a range of guides: the 6-card Check In layout is related to you and your energy bodies, and the second layout is related to getting cards from a range of guides. This second layout, Spirit Guides 5, can be adjusted as you figure out which guides you're responding to most (or if you'd like to start working with specific kinds of guides, you can have a card for them). You get to decide what you're asking for with the cards, which makes them fun and flexible.

Here's the Check In layout:

- Card 1: Your body
- Card 2: Your mind
- Card 3: Your emotions
- Card 4: Your spirit
- Card 5: What needs to be integrated into your energies
- Card 6: What opportunities are coming up

This is a good layout to do monthly or use it as you start the workbook and at the end.

Here's the Spirit Guides 5 layout:

- Card 1: Who you are right now
- Card 2: Angels (including the archangels)
- Card 3: Ancestors and Earth Spirits
- Card 4: Cosmic Connections (star beings, enlightened ones, goddesses, deities)
- Card 5: Outcome if you address the messages received in the cards

Here are a couple of pages to try out these cards and note your thoughts, you might want to keep track of the cards you pull in your regular journal or a separate journal for the cards you pull to track over time.

I lumped some types of guides together due to potential linkages between them. The angelic kingdom gets a card because they are present in all religions and most people will want to work with them, but they are also a broad category. Healing angels and archangels, for example, give different types of guidance. Earth-based guides such as ancestors and earth spirits are grouped together because you're learning to feel your body and your life connected to the planet. The cosmic connections include guides who aren't as related to being in a body. They bring perspectives focused not only on you as a human, but you as a spiritual being having a human experience: they are vast and expansive in guidance and nature.

This layout could be part of a weekly ritual or check-in as you start to work with the guides. You can adjust the beings you call forth for each card based on who you're feeling connected to or the specific type of assistance you need now. It's all up to you and the help you'd like to receive.

Scripts.

Here's a script to help you set up rituals with your guides for general support during a ritual or if you're not sure what to focus on and want guidance about using rituals.

"I call upon all my guides of highest light. Please help me sense what rituals would bring me comfort and support at this time. Please help me release outdated patterns and beliefs using simple rituals so the process is easy and efficiently completed. Please help me open to the wisdom of my guides and my higher self during rituals. Bring me inspiration and ideas for what I can do to strengthen and renew my body, mind and spirit with ease, grace, flow, and joy. I'm grateful for your help, thank you."

Rewrite this script as feels best for you, and then read on for specific ways to release and renew.

....

....

....

....

....

....

....

....

....

....

The next three scripts are specific to the issues and help noted. As always, these are guidelines that you can adjust to best fit your concerns.

Old Patterns or Buried Trauma

"I call upon all my guides of highest light and ask to be surrounded with the energy of compassionate love. I want to release old patterns and buried traumas that are holding me back, whether I am conscious of them or not, and without the need to relive or experience the energies associated with these patterns. I ask for assistance from all my guides and healing angels to release patterns not in resonance with my highest good. I ask that this be done with ease, grace, flow, and joy for all my energy bodies (body, mind, emotions, and spirit), that the energies and patterns released never return to me in this lifetime, and that my energy bodies be healed and sealed following these releases. Please continue to provide support for my physical body as I know the body will take longer to process these releases. I am so grateful for the support thank you."

You can make this specific to an issue you know about, or make it for a concern, such as whatever old patterns limit your financial situation, creativity, loving relationships, or health. Look back at the additional steps shared in Chapter 7 for more details on releasing old patterns, and revise or create an additional script with specifics.

Worries and Anxieties

"I call upon all my guides of highest light and wisdom. I am so worried, so consumed and restricted by these anxieties. I don't know what to do. Please help me. Help me calm and quiet my mind. Help me restore balance to my body. Help me find peace in my emotional state. Please help me trust that things can change, that positive outcomes are possible, that new options and opportunities can appear for me. I would love to feel your presence and know you have my back. Help me trust you, help me trust myself and my ability to create a new future free of these worries, constraints, and anxieties. Thank you so much."

Revise or create an additional script with specifics.

Low Self-Esteem and Self-Worth

"I call upon all my guides of highest love and light. I'm struggling with feeling I'm capable of handling what life is throwing at me now, let alone being able to make my dreams come true. I'm not sure you're around to help me so please make your support and presence known. Help me know I'm worthy of all the love and support you can provide. Help me know my dreams come to me because I can make them come true. I want to stand strong and confident in the knowledge that I can reach my goals and it's worth pursuing them, even as I doubt myself. Please give me the courage and strength to go after what I want despite my inner or outer critics. Help me see a future self who has already accomplished what I'm seeking. Thank you so much for your support."

Revise or create an additional script with specifics.

....

....

....

....

....

....

MORE JOY

BECAUSE JOY IS SUCH AN expansive emotion and energy, I wanted to give you space to explore it more. Feeling joy is one of the fastest and most powerful ways to get more guidance and expand the positive aspects of your life. Check out the playlists at https://julesapollo.com/extras or create your own as a way of jumpstarting more joy using music.

Each time you focus on resolving an issue or releasing a constraint, try to also spend time looking at ways you can feel more joyful in your life. Here's a script to get you started.

"I call upon all my guides of highest light and greatest joy. Please help me feel your ecstatic state more frequently. Help me cultivate practices that will support more powerful joy and free expression as I move through my day. Help me support the people I love to find their creative joy and expansive bliss in their lives as well. Please help me sustain a serene state and peaceful joy even if there is chaos or trouble around me. Help me retain this peaceful joy even as I assist others and work to create a world free of suffering. Help me know that tapping into joy is a portal to expressing more of the light and love of my higher self. I appreciate your aid and support, thank you."

The following paragraphs include suggestions for further exploration of joy and associated beauty, creativity, peace, and serenity.

Movement and Joy.

What kinds of movements have you found to support more joy and better guidance? What activities bring you inspiration and feelings of exuberance or joy? Taking a beauty break to explore a new neighborhood, art exhibit, type of food, garden, or music feeds your creative well, brings inspiration, and an appreciation for life, all of which are fuel for more joy. Creating something is joy fuel as well. What can you explore more?

....

....

....

....

....

....

....

....

....

....

....

....

....

Dreams and Possibilities.

Dreams can be something we hold secret, hidden away from others because they feel fragile. These are perfect for sharing with your guides, and asking for their help to make these possibilities grow and bloom. Ask for help in excavating your buried dreams from childhood that you decided couldn't come true. Look at people you admire and then look for the seed of the dream you have that's like who they are and what they've done. Ask for help to clearly see any dreams you're avoiding because they feel too audacious to think about, let alone share or pursue. Ask for help from your higher self or do the 'future self' tarot reading in Part 3. Try on the energy of when you've accomplished your oldest dream: who are you when your dreams come true?

....

....

....

....

....

....

....

....

....

....

Powerful and Free.

When I talk about feeling empowered, being the 'Queen Me' in *Spirit Guides on Speed Dial*, how does this feel to you? What makes you feel powerful? When have you felt most powerful in your life? If you don't have a lot of examples from your life, who do you admire that you could emulate to feel more powerful? If you don't feel comfortable with the idea of being powerful, if the word has negative connotations for you, substitute the word 'free' for power – when do you feel most free, most alive, most vibrant? How can you bring more of that into your life?

Do monthly or quarterly joy check-ins to see if hanging out with your guides is affecting your everyday reality and baseline emotional state. Track this over time: what is the best way you've found to be buoyantly joyful? How can you bring on more of it? How do you get into a state of joyful creativity and free flowing ideas?

....

....

....

....

....

....

....

....

....

....

....

....

....

....

PART 3

UNFURLING AND EXPANDING

The intent with this section is to give you space to focus on how you can expand your life, what you've been feeling and experiencing since working through this workbook, and how your view of your life and possibilities has shifted with the processes shared in the book.

- How have your ideas of who you are, your capabilities and possibilities, unfurled and expanded since starting the workbook?

....

....

....

....

....

....

....

....

....

- Do you feel the light of your soul, are you sensing your higher self along with working with your guides? What's that like? What new dreams, skills, possibilities are you aware of? How is this changing how you see your current life and future potential?

....

....

....

....

....

....

....

....

....

....

....

....

....

....

- Create an image or collage of who you see yourself becoming as you continue to pursue your dreams and goals with the support of your guides.

- Ask your higher self and guides to help you get guidance from your future self: what comes through? What does she want to tell you, to have you remember? Throw some tarot or oracle cards to help with this. Here's a 4-card layout to start, you can add more cards as needed.
  - Future Self 4 Card Spread
  - Card 1: Who you are now
  - Card 2: What's going on related to your concern or life in general
  - Card 3: What your future self wants you to know
  - Card 4: Outcome and opportunity

- Play with the ideas of 'how good can you let it be' and 'what if' related to a particular aspect of your life or one of your dreams. Expand it even more, be outrageously optimistic and see how expanded you'll allow yourself to be. Ask for help from your guides to make it as big as possible and spend time envisioning how it would feel if your life were better beyond belief. Mind maps and vision boards are perfect for this. Use archetypes or your heroines for inspiration. Call in guides related to your expansive dreams to partner with, you can even create a council that you routinely work with, like a Creativity Council, to sustain your momentum. This approach is particularly powerful if you're looking to create more abundance in one area of your life: money, creativity, time, energy, health, love, career.

- Document your goals and progress or shifts since starting the workbook. How might you work with your guides to efficiently reach your goals through calling in more types of support, asking the guides to take on more aspects of the goals, or getting help to complete your work with as much ease, flow, and joy as possible? How can you approach your goals as a project manager? See Chapter 5 in *Spirit Guides on Speed Dial* for more details on this if needed.

- Have you tried creating an inner sanctuary for dreaming? Which approach worked best? Document your work and date it so you can look back in a few months and note how you've made the process your own. Share details of your sanctuary, draw, sketch or include images. See https://julesapollo.com/extras for a link to Pinterest pages with images for inspiration if this is helpful.

- How can you continue to work with your higher self to understand and access your soul skills and strengths to share your gifts? How might you use these skills to contribute to a better world?

CLOSURE

YOU NOW HAVE THE TOOLS, tips, and scripts to help you partner with your guides to create the life and world you want.

In every message I've channeled, in every private session and course I do, the guides always repeat the same message: how deeply loved we are and how ready they are to help us. I hope you feel all the love that went into this workbook and that's flowing around you now. It's ready when you need it, and it's already with you. I wanted to share a message from the guides as it's so important and powerful. This is the same message that's at the end of *Spirit Guides on Speed Dial*, I think it's so important that I wanted to repeat it here. Read it out loud and then go for a walk or take a long bath and let it sink in.

Archangel Michael shared some thoughts with me on the power of our resilience and the need to share our gifts in these times of chaos on the planet.

Thank you for your efforts, your perseverance, your willingness to get up again after you fall, and the resilience of your heart. It is a thing of wonder to us, for we have rested always in the comfort of the light while you have chosen to be blind to the truth of your beauty, to stumble through the mud, and to be washed anew against the rocks of these times.

Release these final bonds and chains that keep you meek and thinking small. You cannot hide your light now. You cannot convince yourself that your time to act, speak, and share is any time other than now.

Flood your surroundings with the light within you that cannot be contained. That is your path and your mission now. We love you, we hold you, we carry you, we sing to you, we remember you, we see you clearly. We are right here with you, cheering you on. What beauty be this love we have for you.

I can't wait to see what you create with this new support. Reach out and let me know.

A REVIEW REQUEST

IF YOU FOUND THIS BOOK helpful, you can make a big difference.

Reviews are the most powerful way to get books out into the world, especially for self-published authors. Honest reviews help bring this book to the attention of other readers, people who might have been looking for what's shared here for a long time, or who could really use the support provided in these pages.

If you've enjoyed this book, I'd be so grateful if you could spend just five minutes leaving a review on the book's page at the retailer's website where you purchased the book. It can be as short as you like, and you can jump right to the book's review page here:

https://julesapollo.com/review/

Many thanks!

ACKNOWLEDGMENTS

In addition to all the folks I thanked in *Spirit Guides on Speed Dial*, I'd like to thank Choi Messer for her great help in formatting both *Spirit Guides on Speed Dial* and this workbook, and to my early readers for their suggestions to create a workbook.

May this work support creation of a loving, sustainable, equitable world filled with creative joy and peace for all, so be it.

www.ingramcontent.com/pod-product-compliance
Lightning Source LLC
Chambersburg PA
CBHW020233130626
46549CB00005B/1864